FOLK ROOTS, NEW ROOTS

FOLK ROOTS, NEW ROOTS

Folklore in American Life

Jane S. Becker
and
Barbara Franco

MUSEUM OF OUR NATIONAL HERITAGE
LEXINGTON, MASSACHUSETTS

An exhibition organized by the
MUSEUM OF OUR NATIONAL HERITAGE
Lexington, Massachusetts

Supported by the
NATIONAL ENDOWMENT FOR THE HUMANITIES
and the
MASSACHUSETTS COUNCIL ON THE ARTS AND HUMANITIES
OCTOBER 16, 1988 – JUNE 25, 1989

The exhibition will travel to

The McKissick Museum
University of South Carolina
Columbia, South Carolina

August 20, 1989 – November 26, 1989

The Strong Museum
Rochester, New York

March 1, 1990 – July 8, 1990

The Oakland Museum
Oakland, California

August 18, 1990 – November 11, 1990

FRONT COVER ILLUSTRATION: Negro woman quilting, vicinity of Hinesville, Georgia. Photo taken by Jack Delano, April 1941, for the Farm Security Administration. LC–USF 34–43775–D. Courtesy of the Library of Congress.

BACK COVER ILLUSTRATION: *Whole Earth Catalog*, *Foxfire*, and the *Anthology of American Folk Music, Volume I: Ballads*, edited by Harry Smith (Folkways FA 2951). Photo: John Miller Documents.

ISBN 0–9621107–1–x (Cloth)   ISBN 0–9621107–2–8 (Paper)
LC–88–50979

Table of Contents

Lenders to the Exhibition

The Advertising Council, Inc.; *New York*

Albright-Knox Art Gallery; *Buffalo, New York*

American Folklife Center; *Washington*

Archives of American Art, Smithsonian Institution; *Washington*

University of Arizona Library; *Tucson*

Tom and Bunty Armstrong

Gene Autry Western Heritage Museum; *Los Angeles*

Southern Appalachian Archives, Berea College; *Berea, Kentucky*

Birch Tree Group; *Princeton, New Jersey*

Boston Public Library

Buffalo Bill Historical Center; *Cody, Wyoming*

CBS Radio, *New York*

CBS Records; *New York*

California State Railroad Museum Library; *Sacramento*

John C. Campbell Folk School; *Brasstown, North Carolina*

Capitol Records; *Hollywood, California*

Center for Appalachian Studies, Appalachian State University; *Boone, North Carolina*

Martin Cohen

Country Music Foundation; *Nashville*

Basia Dziewanowska

Folk Song Society of Greater Boston

Henry Ford Museum and Greenfield Village; *Dearborn, Michigan*

David Gahr

Woody Guthrie Publications, Inc.; *New York*

Richard and Kellie Gutman

Hake's Americana and Collectibles; *York, Pennsylvania*

The Heard Museum; *Phoenix*

Highlander Center; *New Market, Tennessee*

James Higgins, Higgins and Ross; *North Chelmsford, Massachusetts*

Hindman Settlement School; *Hindman, Kentucky*

Billie Hockett

Jane Addams Memorial Collection, University Library, University of Illinois at Chicago

June Appal Recordings; *Whitesburg, Kentucky*

John Laurent

Paul Lenart

Archive of Folk Culture; Motion Picture, Broadcasting and Recorded Sound Division; Music Division; Prints and Photographs, Library of Congress; *Washington*

Louisiana State Museum; *New Orleans*

Photographic Archives, Ekstrom Library, University of Louisville; *Louisville, Kentucky*

Lowell Historic Preservation Commission; *Lowell, Massachusetts*

MCA Records; *Universal City, California*

McKissick Museum; *Columbia, South Carolina*

John Miller

Mississippi Department of Archives and History; *Jackson*

Linda Morley

National Gallery of Art; *Washington*

National Museum of American History, Smithsonian Institution; *Washington*

Museum of New Mexico; *Santa Fe*

National Council for the Traditional Arts; *Washington*

New Jersey State Museum; *Trenton*

New World Records; *New York*

New York Public Library

New York State Historical Association; *Cooperstown*

State University of New York at Buffalo; *Buffalo*

The Newark Museum; *Newark, New Jersey*

Newport Folk Foundation, Inc.

Penn Center Inc.; *St. Helena Island, South Carolina*

Penn School Papers, Southern Historical Collection, University of North Carolina at Chapel Hill

The Oakland Museum; *Oakland, California*

Oklahoma Historical Society; *Oklahoma City*

The Oral History Center; *Cambridge, Massachusetts*

Peabody Museum of Salem; *Salem, Massachusetts*

Philip Morris, U.S.A.; *New York*

RCA Victor; *Hollywood, California*

R. J. Reynolds Tobacco, U.S.A.; *Winston-Salem, North Carolina*

Rhode Island Black Heritage Society; *Providence*

Rounder Records; *Cambridge, Massachusetts*

Russell Sage Foundation; *New York*

Schlesinger Library, Radcliffe College; *Cambridge, Massachusetts*

Candy Schwartz

The Shelburne Museum; *Shelburne, Vermont*

Richard Spottswood

National Anthropological Archives, Smithsonian Institution; *Washington*

Tennessee State Library and Archives; *Nashville*

Eugene C. Barker Texas History Center, University of Texas at Austin

Andrea Thurber

Tozzer Library, Harvard University; *Cambridge, Massachusetts*

Jeff Warner

Warner Brothers Records; *Burbank, California*

Welk Record Group; *Santa Monica, California*

Foreword and Acknowledgements

I N FOLKLORE CLASSES in the 1960s, the question most
often posed was "Who are the folk?" The very nature of folklore as a discipline involves questions. Folklorists question
their informants—"How do you prepare this dish? How did your
mother sing this song?" Using a recognized methodology,
folklorists have amassed and interpreted data about how communities of people do things and communicate traditions.

This exhibition and publication, marking the 100th anniversary
of the founding of the American Folklore Society in 1888, departs
from the specific methods and subject matter of folklorists. Rather
than taking the folk themselves as its subject, it looks instead at the
larger issue of how folklorists and the American public have used
folk concepts in forming popular culture and national identity. It
examines the sources of Americans' own myths about the identity
of "the folk" and the definitions of folklore, and how these perceptions have served our own searches for personal and national
identities.

The historical approach of *Folk Roots, New Roots* examines a
series of chronological themes that show American fascination
with folk forms and concepts and explains how that fascination
has shifted and been redirected in response to changes in contemporary society.

This project represents a cooperative endeavor involving many
participants. Funding has been made possible by grants from the
National Endowment for the Humanities and the Massachusetts
Council on the Arts and Humanities. Jane Becker, the project
coordinator, has been the guiding force from the initial planning
stages through the final installation. There would be no exhibition
without the impetus given by an initial group of scholars who

thought there should be an exhibition that in some way celebrated the centennial of the American Folklore Society. Anthony Barrand, Boston University; Dillon Bustin, Massachusetts Council on the Arts and Humanities; Hugh Flick, Yale University; Jeanne Guillemin, Boston College; and Robert St. George, Boston University, formed the core of this initiative.

Roger Abrahams, University of Pennsylvania, and Jackson Lears, Rutgers University, served as consultants in the planning phase of the exhibition, lending their respective expertise in the history of folklore as a discipline and 20th-century cultural history. Their help in refining the conceptual framework, locating sources, and critiquing the historical interpretation was crucial to the success of our grant proposals and, ultimately, the exhibition.

Roger Abrahams and Jackson Lears were joined by the other project consultants—Robert Cantwell, Georgetown University and the Office of Folklife Programs, Smithsonian Institution; Rayna Green, National Museum of American History, Smithsonian Institution; Alan Jabbour, American Folklife Center, Library of Congress; Eugene Metcalf, Miami University; and Claudine Weatherford, University of Maryland—lending critical assistance in preparing the grant application for the National Endowment for the Humanities. They have contributed much more than the essays in this catalogue. They have encouraged, brainstormed, helped locate objects; refined concepts and exhibition script; and have shared their excitement and enthusiasm with us.

Since work on this project began two years ago, there are many who have responded generously to our requests for help and offered their moral and intellectual support. Michael Bell, Rhode Island Heritage Commission; Simon Bronner, Pennsylvania State University, Capitol Campus; Elaine Eff, Baltimore Traditions, Baltimore Department of Housing and Community Development; Archie Green; Harvey Green, The Strong Museum; Bess Lomax Hawes, National Endowment for the Arts; Louis C. Jones, New York State Historical Association; Debora Kodish, Philadelphia Folklore Project; Blanche Linden-Ward, Emerson College; Christopher Lornell and Roddy Moore, Ferrum College; Robert St. George and John Saltmarsh, Boston University; William McNeil, Ozark Folk Center; Charles Watkins, Appalachian Cultural Center, Appalachian State University; and David Whisnant, University of Maryland Baltimore County, read and commented on drafts of the exhibition script.

Also, Richard Blaustein, East Tennessee State University; Francis De Caro, Louisiana State University, Baton Rouge; Loyal Jones, Appalachian Center, Berea College; Steven Plattner, Cincinnati, Ohio; Henry Shapiro, University of Cincinnati; Lonn Taylor, National Museum of American History, Smithsonian Institution; John Michael Vlach, George Washington University; Marta Weigle, University of New Mexico, Albuquerque; and Paul Wells, Center for Popular Music, Middle Tennessee State University, shared their own work and expertise with us. Laura Roberts, Wayland, Mass., lent insightful criticism and support, and especially imagination, in the development of the exhibition concept. Special thanks to the staff at the John C. Campbell Folk School, Brasstown, N.C., and the Hindman Settlement School, Hindman, Ky., for their warm welcome and hospitality.

We are very grateful for the cooperation of all of our lenders who have made their collections available for this effort: Joan Bober, Advertising Council, Inc.; Kathryn Corcoran, Albright-Knox Art Gallery, Buffalo, N.Y.; Jennifer Cutting, Douglas DeNatale, and Carl Fleishauer, American Folklife Center, Washington; Eric J. Olsen, Appalachian Collection, Appalachian State University; Archives of American Art, Smithsonian Institution, Washington; Louis Hieb, University Library, University of Arizona; Amy Hay and James Nottage, Gene Autry Western Heritage Museum, Los Angeles; Gerald Roberts, Southern Appalachian Archives, Berea College; Birch Tree Group, Princeton, N.J.; Katherine Dibble and B. Joseph O'Neil, Boston Public Library; Paul Fees and Joanne Kudla, Buffalo Bill Historical Center, Cody,

Wyo.; Capitol Records, Hollywood, Calif.; Phyllis Dubrow, CBS Radio, New York; CBS Records, New York; Ellen Schwartz, California State Railroad Museum Library, Sacramento; and Catherine Carpenter, Ron Hill, and Gladys Rogers, John C. Campbell Folk School, Brasstown, N.C.

Also Charlie Seeman and Chris Skinker, Country Music Foundation, Inc., Nashville; Suzanne Mrozak, Folk Song Society of Greater Boston; Ted Hake, Hake's Americana and Collectibles, York, Pa.; Sally Williams, Tozzer Library, Harvard University; Ann Marshall and Diana Pardue, The Heard Museum, Phoenix; Steven Hamp and Jeanine Head, Henry Ford Museum and Greenfield Village, Dearborn, Mich.; Paul DeLeon and Hubert Sapp, Highlander Center, New Market, Tenn.; Jana Vee Everage and Michael Mullins, Hindman Settlement School, Hindman, Ky.; Mary Ann Bamberger and Mary Ann Johnson, University of Illinois at Chicago; June Appal Recordings, Whitesburg, Ky.; Joseph Hickerson and Gerald Parsons, Jr., Archive of Folk Culture, Library of Congress; Donna Elliott, Exhibits Office, Library of Congress; Sam Brylawski, Motion Picture, Broadcasting, and Recorded Sound, Library of Congress; Elena Millie, Prints and Photographs, Library of Congress; Donald M. Marquis, Louisiana State Museum, New Orleans; David Horvath, Photographic Archives, Ekstrom Library, University of Louisville; Paul Marion, Lowell [Mass.] Historic Preservation Commission; MCA Records, Universal City, Calif.; Catherine Wilson Horne and Sue Hosking, McKissick Museum, Columbia, S.C.; Forrest W. Galey and Albert Hilliard, Mississippi Department of Archives and History; Charles Bennett and Richard Rudisill, Museum of New Mexico, Santa Fe; Meg Glaser and Joe Wilson, National Council for the Traditional Arts, Washington; Carlotta Owens, Charles Ritchie, Andrew Robison, and Laurie Weitzenkorn, National Gallery of Art; Robert Harding and Lorene Mayo, Archives Center, National Museum of American History, Washington; Ulysses Dietz and Margaret

DiSalvi, The Newark [N.J.] Museum; Newport Folk Foundation; Suzanne Corlette Crilley, New Jersey State Museum, Trenton; New World Records, New York; Paul D'Ambrosio, A. Bruce MacLeish, and Kathy Stocking, New York State Historical Association, Cooperstown; Francis J. Mattson and Bernard McTigue, New York Public Library; Bruce Jackson, Center for Studies in American Culture, State University of New York at Buffalo; Richard Shrader and John White, Southern Historical Collection, University of North Carolina at Chapel Hill; L. Thomas Frye and Inez Brooks-Myers, The Oakland Museum, Oakland, Calif.; Kathy L. Dickson, Oklahoma Historical Society, Oklahoma City; Diane Chira and Cindy Cohen, The Oral History Center, Cambridge, Mass.; and Elaine Bukov and Lucy Butler, Peabody Museum of Salem, Salem, Mass.

Also Emory Campbell, Penn Center, Inc., St. Helena Island, S.C.; Susan Strausser and Carl Cohen, Philip Morris U.S.A., New York; Martin Olnick, RCA Victor, Hollywood, Calif.; Barry Miller and Jo Spach, R. J. Reynolds Tobacco, U.S.A., Winston-Salem, N.C.; Frederick Williamson, Rhode Island Black Heritage Society, Providence; Rounder Records, Cambridge, Mass.; Priscilla Lewis, Russell Sage Foundation, New York; Marie-Helene Gold, Schlesinger Library, Radcliffe College; Pauline Mitchell and Robert Shaw, The Shelburne Museum, Shelburne, Vt.; Edwin S. Gleaves, John McGlone, and Wayne Moore, Tennessee State Library and Archives; John Wheat, Eugene C. Barker Texas History Center, University of Texas at Austin; Warner Brothers Records, Burbank, Calif.; Welk Record Group, Santa Monica, Calif.; Harold Leventhal, Woody Guthrie Publications, Inc., New York; Martin Cohen, Belmont, Mass.; Basia Dziewanowska, Watertown, Mass.; David Gahr, Brooklyn; Rayna Green, Washington; Richard and Kellie Gutman, West Roxbury, Mass.; James Higgins, Higgins and Ross, North Chelmsford, Mass.; Billie Hockett, Lexington, Mass.; Dr. and Mrs. Theodore Klitzke, Towson, Md.; John Laurent,

York, Maine; Paul Lenart, Cambridge, Mass.; John Miller, Rehoboth, Mass.; Linda Morley, Manchester, N.H.; Candy Schwartz, Boston, Mass.; Richard Spottswood, University Park, Md.; Andrea Thurber, Springfield, Vt.; and Jeff Warner, Washington.

Many others spent considerable time and effort suggesting resources or culling their collections in pursuit of objects, photographs, and manuscripts that helped us in our research. Special thanks are due Richard Miller, Abby Aldrich Rockefeller Folk Art Center, Williamsburg, Va.; Byron Johnson, Albuquerque Museum; Steve Stanne, Clearwater, Inc., Poughkeepsie, N.Y.; Janet Miller, Field Museum, Chicago; John Cole, Center for the Book, Library of Congress; Jim Gentry, Folk Art Center, Asheville, N.C.; Connie Menninger and Nancy Sherbert, Kansas State Historical Society, Topeka; Bob Webb, Kendall Whaling Museum, Sharon, Mass.; Mike Longworth, C. F. Martin and Co., Inc., Nazareth, Pa.; Robert Bishop, Museum of American Folk Art, New York; Jim Bollman, The Music Emporium, Cambridge, Mass.; Kathleen Baxter, National Anthropological Archives, Smithsonian Institution; Marta Weigle, University of New Mexico, Albuquerque; Peter Filardo, Tamiment Library, New York University; Betty Tyson, North Carolina Museum of History, Raleigh; Jeff Place, Office of Folklife Programs, Smithsonian Institution; Michael Bell, Rhode Island Heritage Commission; Melissa Smith, Rockefeller Archives Center, North Tarrytown, N.Y.; Betsy Kornhauser and Elizabeth R. McClintock, Wadsworth Atheneum, Hartford; Victoria Wyatt, The Burke Museum, University of Washington; Warner W. Pflug, Walter P. Reuther Library, Wayne State University; Nancy Baird, Western Kentucky University Library; Frank and Margaret Adams, Arlington, Mass.; Marsha Baker and Harry Forsdick, Lexington, Mass.; Ann Pugh, Lexington, Mass.; Mike Seeger, Lexington, Va.; and Pete Seeger, Beacon, N.Y.

Members of Folklorists in New England (FINE) have been a constant resource since the very beginning, especially Michael Bell, Dillon Bustin, Lou Carreras, Hugh Flick, Janice Gadaire,

Winnie Lambrecht, Steve Matchak, Linda Morley, Jessica Payne, Katherine Neustadt, Allen Smith, Pat Turner, and Eleanor Wachs. The exhibition slide show was made possible by the contributions of several FINE members—Michael Bell, Dillon Bustin, Janice Gadaire, Steve Matchak, Katherine Neustadt, Pat Turner, and Eleanor Wachs—as well as Cindy Cohen, The Oral History Center, Cambridge, Mass..

Special thanks to the staff of Michael Sand, Inc., who designed the exhibition, especially Alan Ransenberg, Michael Sand, Penny J. Sander, Greg Sprick, and Tom Vanin-Bishop; and to Paul Lenart, who designed and produced the audio-visual and audio components of the exhibition. Their ideas, skills, and imaginations made this a special collaborative effort.

Special thanks go to John Miller for his photography; Penny Stratton for her work in editing this publication; Phil Guecia for meeting a tight production schedule while maintaining his usual standards of craftsmanship; and the staff at the Museum of Our National Heritage: Clement Silvestro, John Hamilton, Gloria Jackson, Robert MacKay, and Jacquelyn Oak. Also staff members Susan Balthaser, who not only persevered through the preparation of this manuscript, but also managed all the administrative minutiae; Millie Rahn, for her unflagging enthusiasm for every last detail; and especially Barbara Franco, who guided all wisely, and with great patience and sense of humor saw success beyond the mistakes and always encouraged the loftiest of visions.

Jane Becker
Project Coordinator

Barbara Franco
Project Director

MUSEUM OF OUR NATIONAL HERITAGE
Lexington, Massachusetts

New England Prologue:
Thoreau, Antimodernism, and
Folk Culture

DILLON BUSTIN

FOLK CULTURE is a conceptual knot of ideas—a mesh of utopian dreams, scholarly theories, popular images, and marketing strategies—all with the recurring theme of anti-modernism. *Folk Roots, New Roots* portrays many of the ways these strands of thought have influenced the ideals of American society. The exhibition begins with the founding of the American Folklore Society and the triumph of industrial capitalism in the Gilded Age of the late 19th century. Initial appeals to folk culture in the United States were made two or three generations earlier, however, when the modern factory system first began to transform the landscape, the meaning of work, and the nature of social relations.

One important source of antimodernism was the philosophy of transcendentalism. This philosophy was developed in Massachu-setts during the 1830s and 1840s, an American version of German and British romanticism. Transcendentalists believed that by proper attentiveness to the senses, human reason, and wilderness, it was possible to discern the spiritual overtones in the clatter of everyday life. Henry David Thoreau was transcendentalism's most outspoken advocate for cultural, as well as natural, conservation. Thoreau's writings show his admiration for folk crafts and occupa-tions, and his abhorrence of recently-introduced alternatives.

In his 1843 essay, "A Winter's Walk," the young Henry David Thoreau described crossing the ice of Sandy Pond in Lincoln, Massachusetts:

Far over the ice, between the hemlock woods and snow-clad hills, stands the pickeral-fisher, his lines set in some retired cove. . . . He belongs to the natural family of man, and is planted deeper in nature and has more root than the inhabitants of towns. Go to him, ask what luck, and you will learn that he too is a worshiper of the unseen. [1]

This passage is a reflection of German *Naturphilosophie*, as well as the romantic notion of *der Volk* as the mystical soul of the nation. This doctrine of *Naturphilosophie* contradicted the Enlightenment by viewing nature not as a predetermined mechanism, but as an open-ended, organic miracle. It was a poetic precursor of the theory of biological evolution. [2] Thoreau, like the European romantics of his day, converted the Enlightenment's curiosity about wild savages into a concern for rural folks closer to home; at the same time he viewed natives as emblems of a spiritual truth rather than as specimens of natural history.

The land extending a mile or two westward from Sandy Pond in Lincoln to Walden Pond in Concord was one of Thoreau's favorite haunts, a microcosm of nature and society that he called the Walden Woods. Here he withdrew in 1845 for his famous two-year sojourn in simplicity and elemental living. In 1846, while Thoreau was preoccupied with his experiment, an English antiquarian named William John Thoms wrote to a London magazine, the *Athenaeum*, to propose a new compound word, *folklore*. Like Thoreau, Thoms had been influenced by German romantic nationalism; he wanted to replace the Latinate term "popular antiquities" with a word of Anglo-Saxon origin. This newly-coined word was quickly accepted in England, and soon gave rise to other similar compounds: folktale, folksong, folk crafts, folk customs, folk culture, and the like. Although these specific terms never entered Thoreau's vocabulary, his awareness of poor marginalized workers and their traditional knowledge was parallel to that of the English folklorists and had the same philosophical source. [3]

In *A Week on the Concord and Merrimack Rivers*, written at Walden and published in 1849, Thoreau wrote: "These modern ingenious sciences and arts do not affect me as those more venerable arts of hunting and fishing, and even of husbandry in its primitive and simple form."[4] Yet as husbandry in its primitive and simple form was transformed into commercial agriculture during the 1840s and 1850s, Thoreau could only intensify his criticism. By the time *Walden* was published in 1854, Thoreau's criticism had turned to outrage, culminating in his tirade against the nearby farmer who was clear-cutting new fields:

> I respect not his labors, his farm where everything has its price; who would carry the landscape, who would carry his God to market if he could get anything for Him. . . . Give me the poverty that enjoys true wealth. Farmers are respectable and interesting to me in proportion as they are poor.[5]

As the cultural historian David Marcell has observed, "Thoreau's vision stood progress on its head and inverted traditional American notions of achievement: the highest and best forms of humanity were the simplest and the least materialistic."[6]

What Thoreau, the testy individualist, was ultimately decrying was the dissolution of Concord and other towns near Boston as traditional communities constituting a spacious, egalitarian society of modest means, local markets, mutual toleration, and open access. Already by the 1840s the values he wished to preserve were embodied more by the poor immigrants from Ireland and Quebec, the subsistence farmers, former slaves, and surviving Indians who shared the woods with him on the margins of town than by the hustling, bustling Yankees of Concord Center. In the "Former Inhabitants" chapter of *Walden*, he lovingly portrayed the previous generation to populate the Walden Woods, their crafts and trades, and wondered why their settlement had disappeared: "Might not the basket, stable-broom, mat-making, corn-parching, linen-spinning, and pottery business have thrived here, making the wilderness to blossom like the rose, and numerous posterity have inherited the land of their fathers?"[7] The philosopher of nature insisted on wildness, but not at the expense of small, faltering hamlets.

Thoreau was unique among the transcendentalists for the ethnographic sketches and detailed descriptions of handcrafts that enliven *Walden* as well as *Cape Cod* and *The Maine Woods*, his travel accounts from the margins of New England. Character portraits like those of the French-Canadian woodchopper, the Wellfleet oysterman, and the Penobscot Indian guide were more than literary diversions; they were serious attempts to challenge prevalent attitudes about worth in society. The admonishments throughout Thoreau's writings are equally against new technologies, new attitudes toward profit and possessions, and new complexities in human relationships. "Where is this division of labor to end?" he asked, "and what purpose does it finally serve?" For along with division of labor comes the parceling out of the countryside and the fragmentation of the self.[8]

Dread of coming change pervades the essay "Walking," which Thoreau read often as a lecture during the 1850s.[9] When he set out walking, Thoreau told his audiences, he invariably headed southwest or west, toward the distant frontier and wilderness. What he did not admit in so many words was his avoidance of the expanding mills and tenements of Waltham, Lawrence, and Lowell to the east and northeast of Concord. In this essay Thoreau not only predicted the invention of the automobile, but also the restructuring of property and privacy that would accompany the rise of industrial capitalism. He feared that nature would be degraded and the factory workers demeaned. Yet he worried that the industrial elite would be spiritually impoverished as well as soon as they forgot how to provide for their own needs with their own hands.[10]

Thoreau delineated all the ideas necessary to motivate the study, collection, and revival of folk arts and crafts. His antimodernism was passionate and eloquent, threads of thought he sent spinning into the future. Thoreau's influence as a naturalist has only grown since his death in 1862, but his early call for cultural conservation has not been widely acknowledged.

In 1888 a group of scholars, museum curators, and philanthropists gathered at Harvard University to form the American Folklore Society.[11] Shortly after the academic study of folklore was formalized in this way, the revival of folk cultural skills began in earnest with the establishment of the Worcester Crafts Center and the Boston Society of Arts and Crafts in the 1890s.[12] During the past century interpretations and adaptations of folk culture have become commonplace. But a return to the radical advocacy of folk communities and folk artists themselves, first undertaken by Thoreau, had to wait until the counterculture movement of the 1960s and the public-sector folklife movement of the 1970s. These kindred movements comprise the latest episode in an account of the folk in America. *Folk Roots, New Roots: Folklore in American Life* chronicles the efforts of romantics, reformers, and revivalists throughout the past century to find in folk culture the inspiration for improved community life.

NOTES

1. In Jeffrey L. Duncan, ed., *Thoreau: The Major Essays* (New York: Dutton, 1972), p. 53. This passage was reworked at the beginning of the "Winter Animals" chapter of *Walden*, and inserted in an account of a walk through the woods from Walden Pond to the center of Lincoln, Massachusetts, where Thoreau was to read a lecture, during the winter of 1846.
2. See Sherman Paul,*The Shores of America: Thoreau's Inward Exploration* (Urbana: University of Illinois Press, 1958, 1972), pp. 1–15.
3. Richard M. Dorson, *The British Folklorists: A History* (Chicago: University of Chicago Press, 1968), p. 1.
4. *A Week on the Concord and Merrimack Rivers* (New York: Crowell, 1961), p. 64.
5. *Walden; or, Life in the Woods* (New York: Crowell, 1961), p. 261.
6. See "Fables of Innocence" in Richard M. Dorson, ed., *Handbook of American Folklore* (Bloomington: Indiana University Press, 1983), pp. 73–78.
7. *Walden*, p. 350.
8. *Walden; or, Life in the Woods*, p. 59.
9. Duncan, *Thoreau*, pp. 194–226.
10. Duncan, *Thoreau*, pp. 194–226.

11. See Simon T. Bronner, *American Folklore Studies: An Intellectual History* (Lawrence: University Press of Kansas, 1986).
12. See also "The Figure of the Artisan: Arts and Crafts Ideology" in Jackson Lears, *No Place of Grace: Antimodernism and the Transformation of American Culture, 1880–1920* (New York: Pantheon, 1981), pp. 59–96.

Introduction

ᙏ   ALAN JABBOUR   ᙎ

H OW ARE THINGS in folklore these days?" I am often asked. Would that I were wise enough to answer! But there may be no single answer. Americans mean many things when they speak of "the folk" and their "lore," and have many different feelings about what they mean. What is more, the layers of meanings and feelings correspond to a host of often contradictory cultural actions at many levels of society. At any given moment, a community is being disrupted by a highway construction project; a generation is learning new forms of popular music inspired by folk creativity at the grassroots; a mass-marketed folk design or cuisine becomes a new national fad; a new joke cycle is making the rounds among businesspeople in airports; a state cultural agency is implementing a new program in folk arts and folklife; a youth is paying attention to the tales and telling styles of his grandmother. Beneath this complexity there may be evidence of a pattern, but it is not easy to explicate the larger rhythms of one's own national culture. Let us at least try to sort out some of the threads of our cultural associations with the word *folklore*, and some of the threads in our cultural history that reveal how we act on our attitudes.

The word *folklore* conjures up many things to Americans. And no wonder: it compounds two venerable English words, each of which has dense textures of association and concatenation. Both words once carried a more general meaning—"people" (folk) and "knowledge" (lore). Displaced from their generalized function, both now evoke a more marginal, yet also a more intimate and informal, message. The recent history of the two words, and of

7

the compound word *folklore*, parallels and explicates the recent history of the arena of culture to which they allude.

Folk rings a bell with two main overtones to an American ear. At one level, *folk* (or, more likely, *folks*) is a word for people; but since *people* crowded it out as the ordinary neutral word, *folk* survives with a more home-grown, intimate, colloquial connotation. *Folks* are us, familiarly considered; and though we are a bit defensive about being "just folks" in homespun, our democratic heritage makes us proud of it, too. At another level, at the suggestion of our scholars, we have borrowed from continental Germanic languages the sense of the word that conveys the academic and popular interest in the ever-receding peasant culture, which an ever-advancing modernity is continually eradicating. These folk are the people, too—but the people as them, not us.

As for *lore*, most Americans—probably most English speakers—sense at some deeper intuitive level its relationship to "that which is learned, taught, and passed along." Lore, thus defined, might theoretically include what we learn in school or study in books. But we normally reserve the words *learning, knowledge,* or most recently *information* for describing the formal and systematic accumulation of knowledge within our civilization. Lore, on the other hand, is informal and traditional in the manner of its conveyance, and it relates not to the nation or mankind as a whole, but to the expressions of more homogeneous groups or particular ways of life. Hence, we may speak of "scientific knowledge," or "information in the computer age," but for more traditional realms of human experience we may refer to "the lore of the sea"—or even "the lore of presidential campaigns." An essay entitled "The Lore of the Library" would not describe a library's collections and the information they contain, nor document its formal structures and procedures; rather, it would recount the stories, customs, and shared intimate experiences that have shaped a library, that make it tick as a traditional human institution.

With such textures layered into its components, it is no surprise that the compound *folklore* evokes many things. Coined by the Englishman William John Thoms in 1846, the word made such headway in British and American society as to appear some 40 years later in the name of a full-fledged national organization. The American Folklore Society, founded in 1888, dedicated itself to collecting and studying the folklore of all the national or ethnic traditions established in America, from the American Indian tribes to the British-American and Afro-American traditions and even ethnic traditions such as those of the French in Louisiana. The progress of the word bespeaks an evolution of cultural attitudes in the 19th century, and a revolution in the formal ways the nation addressed its cultural needs. Fifty years earlier, Americans may have worried about cultural change and loss, even as they embraced the social progress that seemed to be its antithesis and may have been its cause. But in the 1880s, they not only brooded over the consequences of progress (as Henry Adams did when contemplating the cultural transformation fueled by machines), but also organized learned societies to do something about it.

The American Folklore Society exists—and indeed, flourishes—to this day. It has been an important vehicle for the professional definition and redefinition of folklore in American society. Those professional definitions have made their mark on the larger society. We might speculate that every definition of folklore entertained by the professional network for at least a generation has found its way into general parlance, where it secures a cultural niche and thereafter competes with other general and professional senses of the word. A professional folklorist today who corrects certain popular misunderstandings about what folklore means may be in fact correcting the definition used by folklorists of an earlier generation.

But professionals are not the only source of definition for the word *folklore*. Nor are they exempt, in their concepts and definitions, from the influences of the larger society. The words *folk* and *lore* have been part of our language since the time when the only professionals were shamans. This embeddedness, in contrast to the invented vocabulary of modern science, makes it hard for professionals to dictate terms. Further, the term *folklore* designates both that which is studied and the study itself. This trait is shared with other cultural keywords in our civilization, such as *history,* as distinct from the scientific vocabulary, which so meticulously separates the observer from the observed. The blurring of observer and observed bespeaks an immersion of the academic study of folklore within a larger cultural movement in America.

In common American parlance, "American folklore" is likely to refer to myths, legends, and other stories that evoke pioneer days. "Appalachian folklore" often refers to older traditions thought to be preserved in supposedly isolated Appalachian communities. "The folklore of City Hall"—or "the folklore of Wall Street"—is the broad corpus of insider insight and know-how regarding local government—or the financial world—shared usually with other insiders and passed along by conversation and narrative, not in writing. "Folklore masquerading as fact" suggests the negative side of our long-standing ambivalence about the folk and their lore; in this sense, the word is equated with misinformation and ignorance. On the other hand, we encounter "Cajun folklore," "Jewish folklore," or "the folklore of miners," describing neutrally or approvingly the traditions of the various ethnic, regional, religious, or occupational groups in America. This popular use of the word approximates the usage current among folklorists of this generation. In all usages the term maintains its core sense of intimacy, shared experience, and the passing along of cultural knowledge in a personal way. What seems to distinguish the usages is whether the thing contemplated is thought of as present or past, near at hand or far away, something that is ours or something that belongs to others.

It is clear, then, that the words *folk, lore,* and *folklore* are steeped in ambiguities of definition and attitude. On the one hand, they conjure up that which is familiar and intimate; they are redolent of our affectionate feelings about our experiences in groups and networks with shared knowledge and common bonds. On the other hand, it is no accident that these words, which once occupied a more central role in our culture, now designate something felt to be a bit marginal. We may cherish traditional knowledge and view with apprehension the erosion of traditional ways of doing and living, but we also prize our progress from peasanthood, our escape from provincialism, our shedding of the shackles of myth and superstition. The ambiguities of the words faithfully echo the ambivalences in our cultural vision of ourselves.

Let us shift our focus from words to actions. A glance at various periods of American history reveals the same cultural ambivalence we see in the words themselves toward the folk and their lore. On the one hand, folklore is my group's heritage or our common heritage; on the other, the detritus of our advancing civilization — at best, a charming echo of faraway and bygone ways of life, at worst, a hindrance to our knowledge, unity, and progress. Which side of the scale weighs more heavily determines what actions we take.

The actions we take seem to have changed in different periods of our history — not in a constant curve, but in undulating waves and rhythms. Different components of the larger national culture (the educated elite, popular culture, folk culture at the grassroots) interact, yet maintain their separate rhythms and identities. But through all the currents, eddies, and countercurrents in our nation between the 1880s and the present, we can discern a steadily growing formal commitment to the conservation of folk culture. Within the ranks of folklorists, that commitment has taken the form of a growing network of "public-sector folklorists." They occupy positions outside the academy — usually in cultural agencies and organizations at the local, state, or federal level. Not only their ideals but their formal positions call for the conservation of folk culture: preserving it in its home turf, educating the wider public about it, and encouraging public policy to be more sensitive to its inherent values. Though the term *public-sector folklorist* is new, the concept was already in existence in the founding of the American Folklore Society and resurfaced later in activist periods such as the 1930s.

Let us now glance at a few specific periods in American history to get an idea of both the complexity and the suggestions of pattern in our national cultural process for coming to terms with our roots.

The 1880s. Enough time had elapsed since the Civil War to allow new cultural trends to seep through. The 1880s was an era during which the commonest coin of the realm featured the head of an American Indian. If it had been the 1970s, educated Americans would be talking about the need for "roots"; but since it was the 1880s, the impulse found an outlet in such developments as the establishment of the American Folklore Society and John Wesley Powell's launching of the Bureau of American Ethnology at the Smithsonian Institution. The American Folklore Society today is perceived as an academic or learned society, but at its founding it was more inclusive. Commitment, not academic affiliation, was the key ingredient for membership, and the society's mandate was not simply to study but to *preserve* American folklore. Thus the development a century later of a "public-sector" wing of the society to balance its academic wing represents not an innovation but a restoration of mission. The Bureau of American Ethnology dramatized an American paradox: during an era when Americans seemed bent on the destruction of American Indian culture, they also sought in some way to save it. The bureau continued its work until after World War II, when it finally ceased to exist as a formal entity, its mission having been absorbed by, and redistributed to, other networks and organizations.

Shifting from the cultural impulse of the educated elite to the realm of American popular culture in the 1880s, we note that the minstrel stage had waned somewhat, and that popular music was in one of its periodic troughs. The western frontier became a new symbolic realm, just as the brief era of trail drives was drawing to a close. The rise of the cowboy image in national consciousness, like the founding of the Bureau of American Ethnology, suggests a pattern among the countercurrents: heightened change brings about its predictable opposite, a heightened consciousness of the need to preserve.

Meanwhile, back at the grassroots, quite different trends were in evidence. Southern black musicians were beginning to abandon the fiddle and banjo in favor of the piano and guitar. And something called "the rag" was brewing at the folk level a decade or so before its entry onto the national stage.

The 1920s. World War I was over, and the cultural adjustments of the postwar period were under way. The era was dubbed the Jazz Age, and indeed jazz was in the air as a new kind of American popular music. Jazz was also in the air in new ways—radio and disc recordings—representing a revolution in our media of cultural communication. But the same discs that brought us jazz also brought a staggering cultural variety to disparate audiences around the country. There were "hillbilly" records for white southerners and other rural citizens; "race" records for Afro-American audiences; and "ethnic" records for a welter of immigrant and ethnic communities in the United States. If a ministry of culture had dictated a program in support of cultural diversity, it could hardly have done better.

Yet the growing network of folklorists in American universities tended to disparage this outpouring of commercial records and radio broadcasts, so full of both tradition and traditional creative innovation, as modern and tainted by popular culture. Many of them, trained at Harvard, were inspired by a preservationist impulse to save, or at least document, the vanishing ways of life and forms of creativity among the folk. To them, their mission was academic; to us, with benefit of hindsight, they were driven in no small part by other cultural forces in our civilization—renascent state and regional pride ("Our state has the most British ballads in circulation"), nationalism ("Cowboy songs are real American folksongs"), and advocacy for the social and cultural grassroots in American life.

The 1920s was clearly an era when the private sector dominated the public sector, and when local and regional consciousness dominated national consciousness. Thus, like the 1950s, it was an era when folklorists concentrated their energies on enterprises undertaken from the base of the academy. Their chief legacy is an array of publications, but they also laid the groundwork for establishment of an important permanent outpost for folklore within the federal government. In 1928 the Archive of American Folk-Song was established at the Library of Congress, the first office within the structures of the federal government that not only was committed to folklife, but actually used the word *folk* in its name. Its first head, Robert W. Gordon, saw his work as a sort of chair in folk music (a concept commensurate with the 1920s), but the archive's work quickly evolved into the documentation efforts and experiments in new technology for which the archive was to become famous in the 1930s and thereafter.

Meanwhile, as in the 1880s, trends at the grassroots showed an experimental, rather than a conservative, cast. Blacks and whites in the South were inventing and elaborating blues, gospel, and other cultural forms, which became major forces in American life later in the century. Yiddish theater was in full flower in New York City. And a wondrous melange of ethnic groups in California and the Great Basin were busy making the California Hispanic *vaquero* traditions of cattle and horse management their own "buckaroo" traditions.

The 1930s. Paradoxically, the decade of the Great Depression is also remembered warmly as an era of exciting activism in the social and cultural arenas. The alphabet soup of federal agencies included offices with a deep commitment to documenting and celebrating grassroots culture—the many cultural initiatives of the Federal Writers' Project come to mind, or the documentary efforts of Roy Stryker's photographic unit within the Farm Security Administration. At the Archive of American Folk Song, John and Alan Lomax developed an aggressive program for documenting American folk music and folklore, and they quickly gained influence with other agencies as national programs and initiatives multiplied. Public art took on a stylistic cast that evoked the grassroots. Like the 1960s, the 1930s was an era when the cultural focus was national, and when young people with a passionate commitment to democratic cultural ideals were vaulted into positions of relative power in setting the terms of the national dialogue. The cosmopolitan elite had embraced the grassroots.

On the other hand, popular culture turned to more cosmopolitan tastes. Popular music had a somewhat uptown cast, and the world of film seemed less interested in embracing the grassroots than did the workers on the Federal Writers' Project. Meanwhile, back at the grassroots, there was a bit of a waning and consolidating after the creative explosion of the 1920s. Such countercurrents remind us how important it is to look at all aspects of society before generalizing about what is happening culturally in any particular era.

The 1950s. Again, the nation was reconstituting itself after a major war. At the national level there was an intense flurry of passion later referred to as the McCarthy period. The nascent folk music revival, born in the late 1930s and early 1940s as an elite movement associated with the political left, went underground, only to resurface in the hootenanny and coffee house movement later in the decade. The federal commitment to documenting and assisting grassroots culture, so prominent during the 1930s, dwindled back to the lone outpost of the Archive of Folk Song at the Library of Congress, and folklorists again concentrated their efforts on gaining a toehold within the academic world.

Among the cosmopolitan, it was fashionable to intone that nothing of national importance was going on in this quiescent era.

Indeed, this might have been true if by "national" was meant "governmental." But within the private sector, as in the 1920s, important cultural developments were brewing. Folk crafts such as quilting made headway as popular hobbies on a national scale. With the advent of rock-and-roll, popular music underwent a revolution of world-shaking consequence, which proved to be a replay of an American cultural pattern discernible since the early 19th century: black-white cultural interaction in the South, followed by national adoption and adaptation of creative elements of that chemistry.

Meanwhile, back at the grassroots, bluegrass music was coalescing in the Upper South as an updated reassertion of that region's cultural values. And throughout the American Plains, American Indian tribes were synthesizing a new ceremonial and celebratory genre, the powwow.

The 1980s. Just as the cultural landscape of the 1880s changed with the advent of professional and learned organizations, so the cultural landscape of the 1980s is being transformed by new networks of cultural agencies and organizations—arts councils, humanities councils, and historic preservation offices at the federal, state, and local levels, as well as many new museums, historical societies, and cultural centers. The arts, humanities, and historic preservation networks are elite and national in origin, but they have radiated to the state and local level since their breakthrough into national legislation in 1965 and 1966. These new networks represent both a new way of categorizing culture and a new means of doing something about it.

Though attention to grassroots culture was not the impetus behind any of these governmental initiatives in the 1960s, the 1970s proved to be a decade of national insistence on the importance of cultural roots, and professional folklorists were alert in lobbying for inclusion in any formal assistance to American culture. The Smithsonian's Festival of American Folklife, established in 1967 as an annual multicultural folk festival on the National

Mall in Washington, had become by the 1970s both a showcase for folklorists lobbying for formal recognition and a training ground for a generation of "public-sector" folklorists, who went on to secure positions in the growing networks of cultural agencies and organizations around the country. In 1974 the National Endowment for the Arts established a formal Folk Arts Program, and in 1976 the U. S. Congress passed the American Folklife Preservation Act, establishing the American Folklife Center at the Library of Congress. By the 1980s, these federal initiatives had both stimulated and been strengthened by the rapid growth of folk arts, folklore, and folklife programs at the state, regional, and local levels, and the public-sector wing of the American Folklore Society gained equal ascendancy with the academic wing.

The public sector in the 1980s has extolled the virtues of cultural diversity and pluralism, urging individuals to be proud of their folk roots, values, and tastes. The private sector sends the same message. There is wholesale borrowing and adaptation of folk and ethnic design patterns and motifs in popular culture. Regional cuisine is celebrated by the most sophisticated writers and exploited by theme franchises. Pop music seems in a bit of a trough (like the 1880s, come to think of it), but it continues to receive bolstering creative infusions from folk styles and genres—especially Afro-American gospel music. Only a few clouds linger to remind us of our historical ambivalence about the folk and their lore: our fear of drug culture and its insider codes and lore, or the bilingual tug-of-war in the Southwest and southern Florida, where Spanish and English have renewed their historical competition.

Meanwhile, to tell the truth, we are not sure just what is happening now at the folk cultural level in America. But the patterns of our cultural history suggest that new creative forms are emerging there, too. We cannot yet see them clearly, nor differentiate passing fads from cultural transformations—but time will tell.

For now, our hasty glance at various periods of American history will perhaps permit us to close with a general suggestion. Our historical ambivalence toward the folk and their lore plays itself out in many ways on many levels. Happily, for those of us whose commitment to folklore is more unequivocal, the historical countercurrents do not obscure a clear trend over the past century toward a more formal commitment to the conservation of folk culture. Equally important, our cultural multiplicity as a nation insures that no negative attitude toward folklore permeates every level of society at the same time. America seems to foster a kind of creative cultural flow that circulates and reinvigorates, rather than simply discards. The flow of cultural ideas in America is neatly exemplified by the history of the banjo, which has moved from Afro-American roots into both popular music and white southern tradition, carrying and receiving creative ideas as it goes, finding new patrons and conservators even while being abandoned by its earlier custodians. Cultural ideas move synergistically from root to branch, from group to group, from folk to pop and back again, into the hands of our professional priesthood and back out again. This restless recycling of culture so characteristic of our history is set into motion partly by our very ambivalence about our roots. For a system of cultural custodianship, it is messy, like the rearing of an orphan in the homes of kin and friends. On the other hand, to a remarkable degree, it works.

Revealing Traditions:
The Politics of Culture and
Community in America, 1888–1988

❧ JANE S. BECKER ❧

T HROUGHOUT THE PAST century, many of the images and customs connected with our nation and with
being American have been associated with ideas about
"the folk." The songs that we sing, the art and crafts that we admire
and collect, the images that sell our products, even our clothing
and lifestyles—all reflect particular interpretations of folk traditions and folk cultures.

Our American fascination with "folk" has been intertwined with
struggles to define a national culture and identity in a changing
world. As the United States has become increasingly industrialized
and ethnically diverse, social and cultural dislocations and the
increasing complexity of modern life have caused Americans to
seek connections with a perceived simpler, more natural, preindustrial past. In this search, we have consistently turned to
idealized concepts of "folk" to define and sustain notions of community amid rapid and disruptive change.

Many social theorists and historians have drawn on German
scholar Ferdinand Tönnies' ideas about community to explain the
change in social relations accompanying America's industrialization.[1] Tönnies distinguishes between two types of communities,
gemeinschaft and *gesellschaft*. Against a backdrop of economic
change, the movement from small towns to cities and from farms
to factories, *gemeinschaft* ("community") is defined as a society in

which human relationships are based on family, kinship, and other personal networks and in which group solidarity is the ethos. *Gesellschaft* ("society"), on the other hand, is characterized by an artificial grouping of people, competition, and impersonality.[2] It is this notion of *gemeinschaft*, the organic community, that has come to be seen as the essence of the ideal community and folk society.[3] Characterized by mutual interdependence, face-to-face relationships, communal interactions and rituals, self-sufficiency, and homogeneity, ideas about the folk have expressed idealized concepts of preindustrial social and economic relationships. The work values and patterns, social relationships, cultural forms, aesthetics, and physical environments of folk culture have been an intrinsic part of notions of American identity; they remain fundamental to the model of ideal community. Folk images continue to be used to express and maintain changing concepts of community as well as national and group identity.

In 1888, a diverse group of men and women in Cambridge, Massachusetts, joined to form the American Folklore Society (AFS). It was their intent to publish a journal "for the collection of the fast-vanishing remains of Folk-Lore in America, namely: relics of Old English Folk-Lore . . . the Lore of Negroes in the Southern States . . . the Lore of Indian Tribes of North America . . . the Lore of French Canada, Mexico, etc." Their primary interests were ballads, tales, myths, superstitions, and dialects.[4]

The early members of the AFS had diverse collecting interests and represented a variety of backgrounds. They included professors of English such as Francis James Child, historian Francis Parkman, writer Samuel Clemens, psychologist G. Stanley Hall, and anthropologists engaged in studies of Native Americans. Many early members, especially women members, were also actively engaged in social reform. The literary scholars tended to define folklore in literary terms: they used stories, ballads, poetry, jokes, and proverbs as their texts and investigated their origins and evolutions. Those with an anthropological perspective took an ethnographic approach, studying the social customs and beliefs of "primitives." The social activists wanted to help those of less advanced societies in the steps towards civilization. All were interested in recording the survivals of peoples associated with disappearing, less advanced, "backward" cultures untouched by the march of modern civilization.[5] By recording these cultures, they also hoped to preserve the community values inherent in preindustrial societies, whether found in the exotic customs of Native Americans or in the remnants of Anglo-Saxon traditions.

Since the founding of the AFS, students of folklore and folklife have held conflicting notions of "the folk" and "folklore" as they have struggled to define their field of inquiry, its tasks and goals. Folklorists no longer apply the term *folk* only to primitive, isolated peoples whose traditions are endangered by the forces of modernity. Instead, they recognize that every individual belongs to a variety of groups, each of which has informal ways of communicating and customs peculiar to itself.[6] According to this definition, on some level we all have "folk" aspects in our lives. Folklorists also agree on an expanded definition of *folklore* that includes the products of informal communication. Such products may be verbal (stories and songs), or they may be skills and their material results (crafts, tools, utensils). Social customs and the performance of traditional music, dance, and drama are also the folklorists' concern as traditional expressions that are passed on informally and that persist in recognizable but dynamic forms.[7] Similarly, folklorists today have broadened their definition of what constitutes "tradition," recognizing that different groups identify different aspects of their experience as traditional.[8]

Just as the academic definitions of *folk* and *folklore* have changed over the past century, so too have the more popular notions and attitudes that help inform our sense of community. Certain aspects of folk society and cultures, borrowed to help define American culture, have in turn created stereotyped images and notions of folk characters and traditional culture . At the turn of the 20th century, folk culture was seen as an alternative or challenge to the emerging industrial capitalist society. Since then, many ideas concerning folk culture's social and economic orders have been popularized and incorporated into mainstream culture via the media, the arts, and advertising.

The exhibition *Folk Roots, New Roots: Folklore in American Life*, and the accompanying essays, reflect the variety of ways in which Americans have understood their relationship to traditional "folk" culture; how these perspectives have shaped American identities and been used to contend with social, economic, and cultural change; and the process by which "the folk" have been incorporated into mainstream culture. The exhibition explores popular concepts of "the folk" and "folkness," how such ideas are expressed and disseminated, and how such interpretations contribute to changing concepts of community and national identity.

ROMANTIC VISIONS

At the end of the 19th century, folklorists agreed that "the folk" were primitive peoples untouched by the advances of new technology and industrial civilization. Exotic remnants of a life associated with the preindustrial past, folk cultures were in danger of disappearing and rapidly being replaced due to industrialization. Fascination with disappearing cultures and antiquities encouraged many efforts to collect and record the endangered relics of preindustrial cultures so that they would not be lost forever to the inevitable march of civilization. These efforts were encouraged by the founding of organizations such as the American Folklore Society. Of the Indians, these early folklore scholars noted that "it is desirable that a complete history should remain of what they have been, since their picturesque and wonderful life will soon be absorbed and lost in the uniformity of the modern world."[9] The federal government embarked on the scientific study of Native Americans through its Bureau of American Ethnology, established in 1879.[10] Ironically, it was the harsh treatment of these peoples by the government during the course of the 19th century that hastened the demise of traditional Native American culture.

Many Americans took an especially active interest in the culture of America's Indians in the late 19th century. Although native peoples were considered less civilized and lacked the benefits of progress, from a distance Americans could idealize aspects of Native American culture that they missed in modern life. Romantic fascination with Indian life and culture was expressed in exhibitions, manufactured goods, and advertising materials. The late-19th century image of Native American life fulfilled the romantic version of the ideal community. Indians were seen as exotic, self-reliant, full of vitality, stoic, and brave. They had rich communal lives, lived intimately with nature and the natural landscape, and possessed rich spiritual beliefs expressed in colorful and exotic rituals. All these aspects of Indian life contrasted sharply with the environments, relationships, and ethos of modern industrial life.[11]

Romantic images of the Indians reached the public in a variety of ways. The photographer Edward S. Curtis offered images of Indian life through exhibitions and in popular magazines such as *Scribner's*.[12] In his determination to document a culture already disappearing, Curtis created many valuable ethnographic documents; however, he also falsified some by posing subjects in inappropriate traditional costume and creating scenes that reinforced the romantic preoccupation with the Indian as hero and craftsman, living intimately with the natural environment.[13]

Indians and Indian life were also popular sources of commercial images at the turn of the century. Idealized Indian figures hawked tobacco and cigars, and Indian healers sold patent medicines. Beginning in 1882, fierce Indians in William Cody's Buffalo Bill's Wild West Show entertained crowds with reenactments of raids and battles. The railroads, too, both contributed to and made use of the curiosity about Indian culture. Along with the Fred Harvey restaurant and hotel business, the Atchison, Topeka and Santa Fe Railway built a successful enterprise that encouraged tourists to

Hopi women at the Mealing Trough, before 1906. Edward S. Curtis. Courtesy of the Peabody Museum of Salem.

experience the Pueblo culture of the Southwestern Indians. By sponsoring tours through Indian lands; commissioning artists to produce Indian themework for magazines, train stations, and hotels; and amassing, displaying, and selling collections of traditional Indian art and artifacts as souvenirs, the Santa Fe Railway and Fred Harvey brought images of the spiritual and artistic richness of Pueblo culture to many Americans.[14]

Passion for the preservation of antiquities went hand in hand with pride in the scientific and technological advances of the day, revealing the ambivalence that late-19th century Americans felt toward their changing world. At the World's Columbian Exposition, held in Chicago in 1893, Americans applauded science and industry, but also sought to present the old-fashioned and the

Interior of the Fred Harvey Store "Indian Room," Alvarado Hotel, Albuquerque, New Mexico. Neg. 14573. Courtesy of the Museum of New Mexico, Santa Fe.

primitive. "White City" exhibits celebrated the triumphs of technology, and yet revealed the rural pasts of America's peoples in some of the individual state displays. By contrast, the Old World peoples who exhibited in their "villages" on the Midway—the entertainment zone—were presented as exotic and quaint.[15]

Native Americans appeared in both the White City and Midway exhibition areas at the exposition. Under the leadership of Frederic Ward Putnam of Harvard's Peabody Museum of American Archaeology and Ethnology, anthropologists such as Franz Boas, Alice Cunningham Fletcher, and John Wesley Powell created ethnological exhibits of Native Americans that appeared among other displays of Indians from around the world in the

Anthropology Building. According to Major Ben Truman's *History of the World's Fair*, the Anthropology Building was

> one of the most interesting features of the Fair both as regards the curiosities and relics it contains and for the comparative object lesson it presents. All around it are the evidences of the latest steps taken in the world's advancement, while inside the building are the objects that show how the rude forefathers of a thousand tribes delved, dug, and builded.[16]

Many of the Native American exhibits at the exposition were located in or near the Midway, where, with villages of other "primitive" races and groups, they stood as a vivid example of an uncivilized and unenlightened people compared to the vision of progress and grandeur embodied in the classical architecture and technological triumphs of the White City.[17] Americans' ambivalence toward technological progress was rooted in these two views: they reveled in the developments that made possible the wealth and autonomy reflected at the Chicago exposition at the same time that they bemoaned the accompanying problems of urban and industrial life. Unable to fully embrace all the fruits of the new America, Americans responded to these changes with a fascination with what they perceived as endangered—the past, the primitive, and the rural.

SOCIAL AND AESTHETIC REFORM

Nineteenth-century Americans associated folklore with groups of people other than themselves and mourned the loss of such primitive cultures and communities as the Native Americans. By the early 20th century some Americans began not merely to record remnants of an earlier way of life for posterity, but to preserve and integrate aspects of preindustrial communities into modern society. Reacting against modern mechanization and division of labor, these early-20th century reformers believed that preindustrial work processes and handicrafts could effect social and cultural changes, especially among the underclasses of America—immigrants, mountain folk, and blacks. To such reformers, "the folk" were by definition craftsmen and women. Folklore, aesthetics, and social reform merged in the philosophy of the Arts and Crafts Movement.[18] Influenced by the Englishman William Morris, American Arts and Crafts proponents sought to reunite art and labor, handwork and head work, the artist and the laborer—essentially to return to the values, processes, and quality of products of preindustrial labor. Many reformers hoped not only to revive the old practices, aesthetics, and standards, but to recapture the ethos and community—the *gemeinschaft*—in which such work took place.

Handicraft became a panacea for the ills of industrial society. It provided relief from the monotonies of both intellectual work and repetitive factory labor. Advocates of the handicraft revival saw in the craftsman ideal an antidote to modern problems among both white-collar and factory laborers. It helped shape whole, integrated individuals and thus protected society from the dangers of a depressed middle class and a restless, demanding working class.[19] Arts and Crafts advocates also saw handicraft as the basis for aesthetic reform in their considerable efforts to cultivate good taste; they encouraged an aesthetic based on simplicity in design and form, with a focus on natural materials and handcraftsmanship. Social reformers found that handicrafts offered physical, social, and moral benefits as well; crafts made in community offered respite from social isolation and taught habits of industry and thrift.[20] Home production was regarded as a more wholesome occupation than factory work. In promoting craft processes, cultural values, and aesthetics of the preindustrial craftsman, the Arts and Crafts reformers enshrined the artisan as a "folk" figure.

The revival of handicraft often took place in the context of the urban and rural social settlements and manual training schools. Social workers in urban settlement houses stressed the values and work habits of preindustrial craftsmen in their commitment to educate and to integrate immigrants into American life. At Hull House in Chicago, Jane Addams had established a labor museum

Hull House Labor Museum, 1903. Courtesy of the Jane Addams Memorial Collection, Special Collections, University Library, University of Illinois at Chicago.

that featured Old World craft traditions and related these crafts to modern modes of production. Hull House crafts also revealed attempts to inculcate the working-class, immigrant population it served with particular aesthetic values and standards of craftsmanship, to allow expression of the "instinct of workmanship." Crafts were used to strengthen community ties, foster respect, and encourage social relations between generations and between immigrant groups.[21]

In the southern mountains, well-to-do and educated women established settlement and folk schools, where they encouraged what they considered the most valuable aspects of surviving Anglo-Saxon culture expressed in the ballads, dances, and handicrafts of impoverished rural mountain communities. In many cases these reformers introduced new—or reintroduced presumably traditional—crafts, music, and dance. The handicraft revival

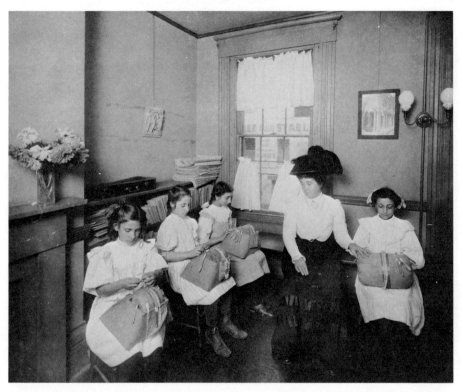

Lacemaking class at Denison House, Boston, ca. 1910. Courtesy of the Schlesinger Library, Radcliffe College, Cambridge, Massachusetts.

movement in the southern mountains was flourishing by the 1930s, and the instrumental Southern Highland Handicraft Guild (founded in 1929) counted many leading social reformers among its founders.

At the turn of the century, Katherine Pettit established the Hindman Settlement School as an educational and social settlement in eastern Kentucky. Drawing on the craft skills of their neighbors, Pettit and her colleagues began their handicrafts program with a basketweaving class taught by local women. By 1904, classes had expanded to include woodworking. Through "fireside industries" the reformers hoped to honor local traditions, preserve family and social stability, encourage useful skills, and raise money for the school. By 1910, local people were entreated to

Bird Owsley, basketmaker, and his wife, on the porch of their house. The Hindman Settlement School's Fireside Industries encouraged craft traditions such as Owsley's, and provided an outlet for local people to sell their handicrafts. Courtesy of Hindman Settlement School Collection, Southern Appalachian Archives, Berea College, Berea, Kentucky.

bring crafts of all types to the school for marketing by Fireside Industries. Olive Dame Campbell established the John C. Campbell Folk School in Brasstown, North Carolina, in 1925 to offer work and education appropriate to life in the mountains. Modeled on the Scandinavian folk schools, the Campbell Folk School offered courses and skills based on shared, local traditions that would enhance economic, social, and cultural life in the mountain communities. The school fostered singing and dancing using indigenous instruments such as fiddles and banjos, but Campbell also introduced Danish dances and instruments borrowed from Scandinavian models. By 1929, local people were employed at traditional crafts, and the school crafts enterprise, which was known

Aunt Cord Ritchie and her husband delivering baskets to the Fireside Industries at Hindman Settlement School, Hindman, Kentucky. Fireside Industries sold oak split melon-shaped baskets and baskets of buckeye split and willow in a variety of forms, as well as handwoven goods. Courtesy of Hindman Settlement School Collection, Southern Appalachian Archives, Berea College, Berea, Kentucky.

for its small carved wooden animals and weaving, flourished through the 1930s.[22]

Many reformers engaged in craft revival efforts encouraged a selected variety of folk traditions among their constituencies that reflected the reformers' preferences for the rural, the natural, the simple, and the organic over the urban, the complex, and the artificial. The reformers' utopian dreams of the self-sufficient, ideal community withdrawn from the modern world of industrial capitalism resulted in their largely frustrated attempts to create economically viable craft industries.

In addition to craft revivals, mountain settlement workers also

Local women delivering baskets to Fireside Industries at Hindman Settlement School. Courtesy of Hindman Settlement School Collection, Southern Appalachian Archives, Berea College, Berea, Kentucky.

fostered English cultural survivals such as ballads and play-party songs (songs that were combined with dance movements in particular games). Ballad-collecting among America's folklorists had first been stimulated by the publication of Francis James Child's collection, *The English and Scottish Popular Ballads* (1882–1898). Later, Katherine Pettit collected songs and ballads and encouraged ballad singing among her constituents at Hindman Settlement School. With George Lyman Kittredge, Child's student at Harvard, Pettit published a volume of Anglo-American ballads she found in the southern mountains. Olive Dame Campbell began collecting ballads in the southern mountains while accompanying her husband, John C. Campbell, on a social survey of the

Animals carved from wood by craftsmen of the John C. Campbell Folk School community. Photo: Werner Kahn. Courtesy of the John C. Campbell Folk School, Brasstown, North Carolina.

area for the Russell Sage Foundation. After meeting Cecil Sharp, a ballad, song, and dance collector from England, Mrs. Campbell and Sharp worked together to locate ballads, and published *English Folk Songs of the Southern Appalachians* in 1917.[23]

Aunt Minde Curtis, at 93 the oldest citizen of Brasstown, North Carolina, when the Campbell Folk School was started in 1925. Ca. 1929–33. Photo: Doris Ulmann. Photographer Doris Ulmann worked among the Campbell Folk School community in the late 1920s and early '30s. Fascinated by mountain craftspeople, her photographs of them are frequently romantic; she often posed her subjects dressed in homespun clothing, with old spinning wheels or other tools of their craft. Courtesy of John C. Campbell Folk School Collection, Southern Appalachian Archives, Berea College, Berea, Kentucky.

Cecil J. Sharp collecting old English ballads and folk songs in the Southern Highlands. In John C. Campbell, *The Southern Highlander and His Homeland* (New York: Russell Sage Foundation, 1921). By permission of the Russell Sage Foundation, New York.

Settlement workers and ballad collectors alike were fascinated by and encouraged aspects of mountain culture that survived from old English traditions. This image of white mountain folk—as isolated bearers of obsolescent English traditions—was marketable to the rest of the nation. Articles in popular magazines made frequent mention of mountain traditions. As the singers of traditional ballads and crafters of traditional arts, the southern mountain people were embraced as an American folk culture that preserved preindustrial values but were comfortably Anglo-Saxon.[24]

CULTURAL NATIONALISM

During the first part of the 20th century, the concept of an American identity was raised to a conscious level. Increasingly, many Americans felt threatened by the burgeoning immigrant population and feared that these new citizens would overwhelm the

Anglo-Saxon traditions and values that were regarded as American. U.S. involvement in World War I also caused Americans to consider the notion of a national cultural identity that would distinguish them in an international context and support the country's new role in world affairs. The response in both cases was a vision of America that was built on a romantic image of the colonial past, with stable social relationships, ethnic and cultural homogeneity, and preindustrial standards of workmanship, craft, and aesthetics. Focusing on images of the American past and "folk" traditions, Americans in the years surrounding World War I created institutions and cultural definitions that reflected a nationalistic vision of ideal community, one distinct from other nations in the world, which was also in distinct contrast to the actual growing diversity of American society.

This retreat to a romanticized colonial past is most frequently recognized in the revival and collecting of colonial architecture and decorative arts, but fascination with early American crafts and old-time music also resulted from similar thinking at this time. Cultural nationalism was expressed in the many new American institutions founded during the 1920s and early 1930s that applauded and recognized the unique and viable aspects of American culture. These institutions presented the objects of the American past as the cornerstones of American culture—Colonial Williamsburg (1926), the American Wing of the Metropolitan Museum of Art (1928), and Henry Ford's Greenfield Village (1929). In each case, these interpretations of American life and culture were based on selected and often romanticized aspects and notions of preindustrial America.

Henry Ford embodied the ambivalence toward change in American culture in the early 20th century. A pioneer in technology and methods of factory production and an agent in the rapid changes taking place in American society, "the man who invented the future" was "now carefully rediscovering the past."[25] His interest was the common man, his crafts, industry, and traditions. He wanted to bring to Americans the story of the families who founded the nation, not the great families of the founding fathers, but the ordinary people and their everyday lives. Ford sought to "reconstruct as nearly as possible the conditions under which they lived," for then "we have a history that is intimate and alive, instead of something in a book."[26] In Ford's preservation efforts at Greenfield Village in Dearborn, Michigan, he reconstructed and furnished buildings and shops that were rapidly disappearing from the American scene. His collecting of tools and other everyday objects reflected his commitment to and reverence for the common American.

Ford's creation of an idyllic and harmonious American past at Greenfield Village was typical of the nationalistic vision of American culture that emerged in response to the tensions of modern life in the years surrounding World War I. At Greenfield Village there were no strikes or class and ethnic tensions because there was no diversity to generate conflict among the community's "dwellers."[27] Henry Ford's "folk" were quintessentially Anglo-Saxon. Ford appreciated folk tradition as an integral part of the common man's culture, but the cultural traditions that he wanted to revive were his perceptions of Anglo-Saxon American traditions. From New England he imported an old-time dancing master to teach the two-step, contradances, quadrilles, and waltz and gavotte. Such dances were "typically American and provided much greater opportunity for social training than the more modern dances"; in addition, they were "of greater value than mere recreation."[28] Along with this dance revival, Ford also encouraged traditional musicians. Throughout the 1920s, he sponsored old-time string bands, dance bands, and fiddling conventions, summoning traditional fiddlers such as Mellie Dunham of Maine. Ford's enthusiasm for Anglo-Saxon culture had a dark side, however, that was both anti-Semitic and exclusive of other ethnic traditions.

The "discovery" and defining of American folk art during the late 1920s and early 1930s took place within the social and cultural

Uncle Jimmy Thompson, fiddler from Martha, Tennessee, a winner in one of Henry Ford's fiddling conventions, 1926. Photo: Caufield and Shook. Courtesy of the Caufield and Shook Collection, University of Louisville Photographic Archives.

context of America's emergence as a world industrial power and its growing ethnic diversity. Modern artists who rejected imitations of European styles felt compelled to establish a unique New World cultural identity; the discovery of the paintings, carvings, hooked rugs, and weathervanes that came to be defined as American folk art satisfied the needs of modern artists searching for a peculiarly American artistic tradition on which to build. The same objects appealed as well to the nationalistic and historical preferences of conservative Americans in the early 20th century. The definition of folk art, codified by such collectors as Holger Cahill, was invested with nationalistic and romanticized historical associations. Folk art was primitive in form and style, the product of untrained

Jugoslav string orchestra and singers at the Buffalo Arts and Crafts of the Homelands Exhibition in 1919. Traditional performing arts were also a part of the homelands exhibitions. From Allen Eaton, *Immigrant Gifts to American Life* (New York: Russell Sage Foundation, 1932). By permission of the Russell Sage Foundation, New York.

artists and craftsmen of the preindustrial 17th, 18th, and early 19th centuries—the common men of a great democratic nation.[29]

In striking contrast to this focus on the colonial, Anglo-Saxon roots of American culture, some social reformers did not feel threatened by the ethnic diversity that increasingly characterized American society. Instead, they saw the immigrant contribution to America's cultural, social, and political life as important to national identity and encouraged a vision of America as a nation of many peoples. These reformers organized "homelands" expositions and exhibitions, international folk festivals that exhibited the craft work and native traditions of America's newest citizens. Their goal was to foster respect and tolerance among various ethnic groups . At the Newark Museum in 1916, a New Jersey textiles exhibition included within it a "Homelands Exhibit" featuring articles made in the home countries of immigrant families, lent through the Newark schools. Children visiting this exhibition were

Polish, Hungarian, and German booths at the Homelands Exhibit at the New Jersey State Museum in 1930. From Allen Eaton, *Immigrant Gifts to American Life* (New York: Russell Sage Foundation, 1932). By permission of the Russell Sage Foundation, New York.

taught "how the poorest immigrants from a distant land may have talents and ideals of art capable of transforming crude articles of daily use into things of beauty," and visitors were "made conscious that with the coming of peasants from Europe the virtues of the past still live among us."[30] Subsequently, an important series of Exhibitions of Arts and Crafts of the Homelands, held in Buffalo, Rochester, and Albany, New York, in 1919, provided a model for later homelands events. Undertaken as a joint Americanization effort by the state of New York and the American Federation of Arts, these exhibitions featured the art and crafts of the Old World, craftsmen demonstrating their skills, and native music and dance.[31]

THE COMMON MAN

The blatant nationalism of the 1920s, based on a sanitized Anglo-American past, gave way in the Depression years to the struggle to define a unified national identity based on the discovery and celebration of the "common man" during the 1930s. Against the backdrop of economic depression, Americans strove to adapt to a way of life that did not rely on material or industrial wealth.[32] The philosophy behind the New Deal and its cultural projects disseminated an image of the common man and everyday life that was more pluralistic and included past and present folk traditions and the styles and customs of small-town life. As a result, the products created out of "real experience" came to be highly valued.[33] The folk traditions that provided the basis of the life of the common man were no longer limited to rural, isolated communities among Anglo-Saxon, agrarian peoples. Rather, folk culture was to be found in the lives of a much broader sample of Americans, which now included industrial workers, immigrants, and city dwellers. While folk culture became more inclusive of urban and current traditions, the vision of community that it served still reflected the values, ways of life, and ethos of the vanishing small town.

The government's New Deal programs often promoted the collection and documentation of many aspects of American life and culture. Photographs of rural Americans taken for the Resettlement and Farm Security administrations focused on everyday life and documented a variety of folk traditions as living phenomena. Under the direction of Roy Stryker in the historical section of the Farm Security Administration, accomplished photographers such as Walker Evans and Dorothea Lange captured America's common people, showing families, crafts, farms, music, community and religious life, foodways, and children's traditions.[34] The government sent professional folklorists to tour the American South, collecting and recording folksongs for the Library of Congress and the Works Progress Administration (WPA). Leading one major folk music-collecting expedition through the South in 1939, Herbert Halpert brought with him a sound truck equipped to record musical traditions for posterity.[35] The Federal Writers' Project's American Guide Series encouraged tourism by publish-

Jorena Pettway and daughter of Gee's Bend, Alabama, make chair covers out of bleached flour sacks and flower decorations from paper, 1939. The chairs are also examples of Pettway's work. Photo: Marion Post Wolcott. LC-USF 33-30353-M2. Courtesy of the Library of Congress.

ing state guide books, which focused on the living culture and folklore of specific places as opposed to relics of the disappearing past. Writers were instructed to use people rather than books as their sources for gathering folklore about Indian legends, supernatural tales, festivals, local music, costumes, holidays, foodways, religious customs, and community gatherings.[36] These collections introduced regional and occupational groupings for folklore study. Written for the general public, the folklore collections and the guide books stressed human and contemporary rather than academic and antiquarian values.[37]

The government was only one sector that appropriated "the folk" during this period. For the American Left, workers were the common man and the folk. Various groups and individuals associated with the labor movement of the 1930s identified folk

Zilphia Horton leads striking Chattanooga hosiery workers in song, 1940s. Zilphia Horton, wife of Highlander Folk School founder Myles Horton, collected many songs from people in the area, some of which were used in organizing efforts. She compiled and edited *Labor Songs* in 1939. Courtesy of Highlander Center Archives, New Market, Tennessee.

music as the songs of working people and native social consciousness as the source of their message. Radicals and labor organizers used folk music, portrayed as the songs of *the people*, to unite workers into communities mobilized to achieve economic and social rights. At labor schools in the South, hymns and traditional songs often provided the basis for protest songs. The folk revival among radicals centered on performers such as Woody Guthrie (the Dustbowl Balladeer) and the Garland clan, a radicalized southern folk family.[38] Many of the songs collected at such labor and civil rights centers as the Highlander Folk School in Tennessee were brought north by workers and singers such as Pete Seeger and Woody Guthrie, and disseminated to urban organizers through groups like the Almanac Singers.[39]

Pete Seeger, left; and Woody Guthrie, right, 1940s. Courtesy of the Library of Congress.

The original Almanacs, organized in 1940, included Pete Seeger, son of a prominent ethnomusicologist, Charles Seeger; Lee Hays, an organizer at a labor school in the South; and Millard Lampell, a writer.[40] Seeger met Woody Guthrie in 1940 at a benefit for migrant workers in New York City, and the next year Guthrie

The Almanac Singers: (left to right) Woody Guthrie, Millard Lampell, Bess Hawes, Peter Seeger, Arthur Stern, and Sis Cunningham. Courtesy of Woody Guthrie Publications, Inc., New York.

joined the Almanacs. The Almanac Singers were accomplished performers who wrote their own material or used material from the radical organizing movements in the South. They toured the country, bringing their social and political ideology to the people through their songs.[41]

Although the Almanac Singers disbanded during World War II, some of the members were active in People's Songs, Inc., which continued the effort to bring music to the labor movement, particularly in the form of the Almanacs' tradition of "hootenannies." Hootenannies offered a variety of musical forms, usually carrying social and political messages, introduced new performers, and encouraged audience participation. These audiences were composed of young people who found that "a hootenanny communicates music, ideas, and a sense of the real America to them."[42]

CONSUMERISM AND MASS COMMUNICATION

With the communications boom of the 1940s and 1950s, folk images and traditions were increasingly disseminated through mass media and incorporated into popular culture. Except for the labor movement's political use of folk songs, folk traditions and identities rarely suggested alternatives to the dominant social, economic, and political structures after the 1930s. "The folk" had been incorporated into the consensual image of America and Americans.

This same dramatic rise in mass communication and consumption, however, provided new opportunities for the incorporation of "folk" images in the American identity. Folk materials were made visible and audible to more and more Americans through radio and television programming, and the folk models and heroes that reflected these values were brought into American homes through new technology and consumer goods. Although "folk" still embodied community, classlessness, craftsmanship, and authenticity, it was becoming transformed into a commodity that was artificial, commercial, and mass-produced.

In the 1950s, the folk dominated the field of entertainment. The cowboy as folk hero reflected Americans' romantic vision of the West and of western life of an earlier era. William Cody's version of the cowboy—a courageous adventurer winning the West from the savage Indians—had dazzled the public with his riding, roping, and shooting skills in the popular Wild West Shows as early as 1882.[43] In the 1920s, the radio and recording industries had begun to promote a number of popular "singing cowboys," such as Carl Sprague, Jules Vern Allen, and Jimmie Rodgers. Not only were these cowboys independent, masculine, virtuous, and courageous, they were also musically talented. Many of the early country singers promoted by radio shows and recording companies, such as Gene Autry, adopted western dress and the cowboy character.[44] Hollywood created many cowboy heroes of its own (based on figures such as Tom Mix, popular in the 1920s and 1930s), who combined the image of the cowboy as stuntman with that of entertainer. With the emergence of sound films, it was the Gene Autrys, the singing cowboys, who began to bring their talents and personalities to the screen.[45]

Gene Autry with Champion. Courtesy of the Country Music Foundation, Inc., Nashville.

Many manufacturing companies capitalized on the cowboy as a children's hero to help sell their products. Cereal companies had begun sponsoring cowboy rodeo shows in the 1930s, and sold cereal by offering Tom Mix cowboy paraphernalia in exchange for

Cowboy costumes were popular items for children in the 1940s and '50s. Courtesy of John Miller, Rehoboth, Massachusetts.

"When I hear America singing, the Weavers are there," said Carl Sandburg. In the 1950s the Weavers helped to launch a folk music revival in cities and towns all over the nation, popularizing the music of America's folk. Photo: John Miller Documents. Private collections.

coupons. Other companies such as Quaker Oats and General Mills also pitched the cowboy image toward children. By the 1950s, radio, television, and movies presented the cowboy as an exemplary hero, model friend, and benign authority figure, exhorting children to virtuous and moral behavior while reaping the benefits of advertising products to an increasing population of child consumers. The image of the masculine, rugged cowboy was used to attract adult consumers as well, most notably by companies such as Philip Morris, which sold Marlboro cigarettes.[46]

Cowboy crooners were not the only folk music entertainers. In the 1950s, folk song groups and individual folk entrepreneurs became very popular. Although many of these performers had roots in the radical folk song efforts of the 1930s and 1940s, overt political content was for the most part absent in the 1950s music. The Weavers, organized in 1949, consisted of former members of the politically activist People's Songs, Inc.: Pete Seeger, Lee Hays, Fred Hellerman, and Ronnie Gilbert. Signed by Decca Records, the Weavers were a commercial success in the few years before their success was cut short by blacklisting after Senator Joe McCarthy embarked on a campaign to expose disloyalty and involvement in Communist conspiracy. In fact, most of the folksingers associated with the Left went underground during the McCarthy era; a few, such as Burl Ives, who cooperated with the House Un-American Activities Committee and repudiated their earlier radicalism, enjoyed commercial success during this time. During the 1950s, the Weavers made a number of apolitical recordings. Some of their music, arranged by Gordon Jenkins and backed by his orchestra, sounded much different than earlier renditions by the Almanac Singers, and they brought to light and popularity their versions of many of the songs sung by Leadbelly and Woody Guthrie, such as "Goodnight Irene" and "So Long, It's Been Good to Know You."[47] When the harbingers of a new generation of folk music without the tinges of 1930s radicalism emerged at the end of the decade, the urban folk music revival was launched. In 1958, Capitol Records signed three clean-cut young men who called themselves the Kingston Trio. Their version of the southern murder ballad "Tom Dooley" initiated a commercial folk music revival.

GRASSROOTS AND THE FOLK REVIVAL

The grassroots movements of the late 1950s, 1960s, and early 1970s reflected the alienation of some Americans, especially youth, from the social, political, and cultural climate of the postwar period.[48] Young Americans sought simplicity and honesty in the objects of their everyday lives, and rejected the consumerism and display that characterized life in the prosperous postwar years. Often this meant a return to the handmade and the organic. The

Many young adults in the 1960s and '70s replaced the artificial and mass-produced consumer goods popular in the 1950s with handmade items of natural materials and simple design. Photo: John Miller Documents. Private collections.

elaborately hand-embroidered blue jeans, macrame jewelry, tie-dyed fabrics, and handmade pottery—as well as the fetish for natural foods and materials—are but a few examples of a new aesthetic that drew upon folk cultures and replaced the futuristic taste for plastic and artificial products of the 1950s.

The *Whole Earth Catalog* series, which issued its first volume in 1969, were publications that embodied American desires for self-sufficiency and independence from the corporate structures that effectively ruled their lives. The *Whole Earth Catalogs* promoted a philosophy of personal independence and power through the use of preindustrial goods and skills.

> We are as gods and might as well get good at it. So far remotely done power and glory—as via government, big business, formal educa-

Useful and traditional skills and arts offer personal power, self-sufficiency, and a means of individual expression for peoples of all ages in all types of communities and cultures. During the 1960s and '70s, traditional skills were taught and celebrated in publications such as *Foxfire* and *The Whole Earth Catalog*, while many people listened to music made by America's folk. Photo: John Miller Documents. Private collections.

tion, church—has succeeded to the point where gross defects obscure actual gains. In response to this dilemma and to these gains a realm of intimate, personal power is developing—power of the individual to conduct his own education, find his own inspiration, shape his own environment, and share his adventure with whoever is interested.[49]

Some Americans reacted to the exploitation of the natural environment and the products that characterized prosperous, industrial America. The ecology movement fought for clean water, earth, and air. Naming industry as the villain in the pollution of natural resources, individuals sought to escape the overindustrialized and artificial world by returning to the land, relying on a responsible use of natural resources and processes as the basis for existence. The back-to-the-land and ecology movements reflected a vision of an ideal relationship between man and the earth, a relationship associated with preindustrial folk (often Native Americans).

Folk music as a vehicle of social protest was at the core of the 1960s folk music revival. Whether linked to environmental, labor, or civil rights causes, young musicians such as Joan Baez, Bob Dylan, and Peter, Paul, and Mary continued the Guthrie and Seeger traditions, using folk music to bring the message to the people. Rejecting the commercialized "folk music" of their immediate predecessors, some young musicians of the 1960s folk revival turned instead to the more authentic styles and sounds of rural folk in the 1920s, 1930s, and 1940s, and based their music on the sounds of southern mountain and black blues singers. Under the name the New Lost City Ramblers, Mike Seeger, John Cohen, Tom Paley, and, later, Tracy Schwartz sought to recreate the sound, style, look, and ethos of the hillbilly string bands of the 1920s and 1930s.[50]

The focus on human and civil rights in the 1960s, along with an increasing interest exhibited among university scholars in the neglected groups in American history, encouraged a growing acceptance of America as a pluralistic society. This increasing tendency to acknowledge the variety and validity of distinct groups was reflected in the establishment of the Smithsonian's Festival of American Folklife, which celebrated the cultural expressions of a wide array of folk groups and geographical regions. The federal government has continued to encourage a broader understanding of the nature of folk and traditional materials through the medium of the festival, launched by professional folklorists in 1967.

COMMUNITY ROOTS

As Americans have moved toward a recognition and acceptance of themselves as a nation of diverse groups of people with a variety of traditions, they have more self-consciously expressed and cele-

Family photograph from the Olivia Johns Rice Collection. "On the left is Carrie and Ernest and then Mamma and little John and Freddie sits by Mamma's feet and then Papa and Marion and then little Sarrah and Blanche. Mamma's so sorry Sarrah had her hair cut before she had her picture taken . She looks like a boy." Courtesy of the Rhode Island Black Heritage Society, Providence.

brated ethnicity through many contemporary efforts to discover, define, preserve, and express images of community life. Black Americans' struggles for civil rights and economic justice, cultural recognition, and racial pride have encouraged reclamation of their history and traditions. Examples set by black heritage projects have stimulated similar undertakings by other ethnic groups. The convergence of such projects with the Bicentennial celebration of the mid-1970s also generated other investigations of history and tradition. The fact that many Americans participate in ethnic festivals and displays of cultural heritage suggests that they value the preservation and maintenance of their own cultural pasts. Interest in family history, community history, and historic preservation demonstrates similar concerns and pride in personal, familial, cultural, and community "roots."

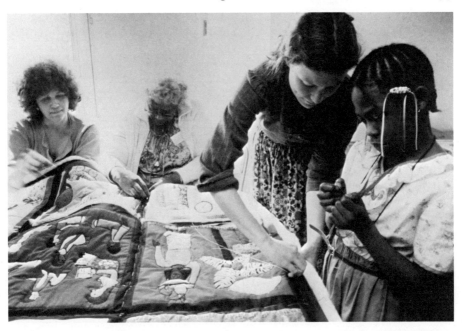

At the Oral History Center in Cambridge, Massachusetts, oral history is used to foster knowledge, respect, and community among peoples of diverse ages and ethnicities. Here women work together assembling a quilt of squares that express their life stories. Photo: Bonnie Burt. Courtesy of the Oral History Center, Cambridge, Massachusetts.

The ordinary, the intimate, and the local are still identified as "the folk." Living in a world of sophisticated technology, politics, and bureaucracy, we still seek to give meaning to our lives and perhaps seek an alternative model of living by maintaining and reviving folk traditions. Using interpretations of traditional culture, we continue to search for ways to identify ourselves as groups and as members of particular communities. In searching for cultural roots, Americans today, as in the past, look to folk roots for meaning about who we are or who we should be, for as Barre Toelken writes, "folklore comes early and stays late in the lives of all of us. In spite of the combined forces of technology, science, television, religion, urbanization, and creeping literacy, we prefer our close personal associations as the basis for learning about life and transmitting important observations and expressions."[51] The notion of "folk" continues to provide a wealth of interpretations and solutions as we as Americans negotiate our way through the changes of past, present, and future. The traditions we seek to preserve and uphold, and the ways in which we interpret them, reflect our own sense of the past and contemporary life.

NOTES

1. The meanings of community in America and the use of Tönnies' typology is the subject of Thomas Bender's *Community and Social Change in America* (New Brunswick, N.J.: Rutgers University Press, 1978). For Tönnies, see Ferdinand Tönnies, *Gemeinschaft und Gesellschaft (Community and Society)*, [1887] trans. and ed. Charles P. Loomis (New York: Harper, 1963).
2. Bender, *Community and Social Change*, p. 17.
3. Robert Redfield applies Tönnies' typology to folk and urban culture in "The Folk Society," *American Journal of Sociology* 52 (January 1947): pp. 293–308 and *The Little Community* (Chicago: University of Chicago Press, 1955).
4. William Wells Newell, "On the Field and Work of a Journal of American Folklore," *Journal of American Folklore* 1 (April-June 1888): 3.
5. Folklorists have become increasingly interested in the history of the field and the founders of the American Folklore Society. Several dissertations treat the subject: William K. McNeil, "A History of American Folklore Scholarship Before 1908" (Ph.D. dissertation, Indiana University, 1980); Rosemary Zumwalt, "American Folkloristics: The Literary and Anthropological Roots" (Ph.D. dissertation, University of California at Berkeley, 1982); and Susan Dwyer-Schick, "The American Folklore Society and Folklore Research in America, 1888–1940" (Ph.D. dissertation, University of Pennsylvania, 1979). Several essays in Richard Dorson's volume, *Handbook of American Folklore* (Bloomington: Indiana University Press, 1983), look historically at the study and interpretation of folklore in the United States. Richard Bauman, Roger Abrahams, and Susan Kalcik's "American Folklore and American Studies," *American Quarterly* 28 (Bibliography Issue, 1976): 360–377, surveys the intellectual history of folklore studies. On the early American Folklore Society and founding members, see also Simon J. Bronner, *American Folklore Studies: An Intellectual History* (Lawrence: University Press of Kansas, 1986) and Bronner, ed., *Folklife Studies from the Gilded Age: Object, Rite and Custom in Victorian America* (Ann Arbor: UMI Research Press, 1987).
6. See especially Alan Dundes, "The American Concept of Folklore," *Journal of the Folklore Institute* 3 (December 1966): 226–249.
7. Richard Dorson, ed., *Folklore and Folklife: An Introduction* (Chicago: University of Chicago Press, 1972), pp. 2–5; and Barre Toelken, *The Dynamics of Folklore* (Boston: Houghton Mifflin Co., 1979): p. 32. See also Dundes, "American Concept of Folklore."
8. Dell Hymes, "Folklore's Nature and the Sun's Myth," *Journal of American Folklore* 88 (1975): 354.
9. Newell, "On the Field and Work," p. 6.
10. For a thorough study of the development of anthropology at the Smithsonian and the Bureau of American Ethnology see Curtis M. Hinsley, Jr., *Savages and Scientists:*

The Smithsonian Institution and the Development of American Anthrolopology, 1846–1910 (Washington, D.C.: Smithsonian Institution Press, 1981). Hinsley looks at the anthropologists as moralists and scientists; his work includes valuable interpretations of BAE scientists such as John Wesley Powell, James Mooney, and Frank Hamilton Cushing.

11. An excellent overview of romantic images of the Native American at the turn of the century is provided by William H. Truettner, "Science and Sentiment: Indian Images at the Turn of the Century," in Charles C. Eldredge, Julie Schimmel, and William H. Truettner, *Art in New Mexico, 1900–1945: Paths to Taos and Santa Fe* (Washington, D.C.: National Museum of American Art, Smithsonian Institution; New York: Abbeville Press, 1986): pp. 17–41. See also Robert F. Berkhofer, Jr., *The White Man's Indian: Images of the American Indian from Columbus to the Present* (New York: Knopf, 1978).

12. For example: Edward S. Curtis, "Vanishing Indian Types: The Tribes of the Southwest," *Scribner's* 39 (May 1906): 513–529 and "Vanishing Indian Types: The Tribes of the Northwest Plains," *Scribner's* 39 (June 1906): 657–671.

13. Curtis published his work in a monumental 20 volumes and portfolios, entitled *The North American Indian*, (Cambridge, Mass., 1907–1911; Norwood, Conn., 1911–1930). Important studies and interpretations of Curtis's work and role include essays by A. D. Coleman and T. C. McLuhan in *Portraits from North American Indian Life: Edward S. Curtis* (New York: Promontory Press, 1978); and Christopher Lyman, *The Vanishing Race and Other Illusions: Photographs of Edward S. Curtis* (Washington, D.C.: Smithsonian Institution Press, 1982).

14. The story of the Atchison, Topeka and Santa Fe Railway and the Fred Harvey enterprises is told in Keith L. Bryant, Jr., "The Atchison, Topeka and Santa Fe Railway and the Development of the Taos and Santa Fe Art Colonies," *Western Historical Quarterly* 9 (October 1978): 437–454; Bertha Dutton, "Commerce on a New Frontier: The Fred Harvey Company and the Fred Harvey Fine Arts Collection," in Christine Mather, ed., *Colonial Frontiers: Art and Life in Spanish New Mexico, The Fred Harvey Collection* (Santa Fe: Ancient City Press, 1983); T.C. McLuhan, *Dream Tracks: The Railroad and the American Indian, 1890–1930* (New York: Abrams, 1985); Diane H. Thomas, *The Southwestern Indian Detours* (Phoenix: Hunter, 1978); Truettner "Science and Sentiment"; and Marta Weigle's unpublished paper, "Ethnic Tourism: The Santa Fe Railway and the Fred Harvey Company Manufacture and Market Southwest Culture." (Paper delivered at the Annual Meeting of the American Studies Association, New York City, 22 November 1987.)

15. Justus D. Doenecke, "Myths, Machines and Markets: The Columbian Exposition of 1893," *Journal of Popular Culture* 6 (1972): 538.

16. Major Ben Truman, *History of the World's Fair* (Philadelphia: Mammoth, 1893), p. 262.

17. In his introduction to *Folklife Studies from the Gilded Age,* Simon Bronner discusses the display of folk peoples and the role of folklore at the Columbian Exposition of 1893, popularly known as the Chicago World's Fair. Robert Rydell's *All the World's A Fair: Visions of Empire at American International Expositions, 1876–1916* (Chicago: University of Chicago Press, 1984) examines American attitudes toward race, evolution, and progress as seen in the ethnological exhibitions at expositions around the turn of the century. Rydell's work is a valuable study of the relationship between scientific and public attitudes toward race and culture.

18. They also merged in the philosopy and person of William Morris, whose ideas about art, culture, and socialism and whose work as a designer fueled the Arts and Crafts Movement in Britain. His interest in Scandinavian folklore resulted in the translation of several Icelandic sagas. Comparing the 12th-century Nordic society with the self-interested one in which he lived, Morris found much to admire in the Nordics' courage, simplicity, and independence. On William Morris, see Edward P.

Thompson, *William Morris: Romantic to Revolutionary* (New York: Pantheon Books, 1976).

19. In his study of antimodernism around the turn of the century, *No Place of Grace: Antimodernism and the Transformation of American Culture, 1880–1920* (New York: Pantheon Books, 1981), Jackson Lears examines the ambivalence of middle-class Americans toward their changing world, manifested in the Arts and Crafts Movement, and the prevalent interest in medieval and primitive cultures and spiritual experience.

20. The intellectual and cultural manifestations of the Arts and Crafts Movement are the subject of Eileen Boris's *Art and Labor: Ruskin, Morris and the Craftsman Ideal in America* (Philadelphia: Temple University Press, 1986).

21. Jane Addams discusses the Labor Museum and goals of the settlement house in her *Twenty Years at Hull House* (New York: Macmillan, 1910; New York: New American Library, 1981). Other important discussions of Jane Addams include Boris, *Art and Labor,* and Jean B. Quandt, *From the Small Town to the Great Community* (New Brunswick: Rutgers University Press, 1970), pp. 86–101. Quandt discusses Addams's ideas about work and culture and the role of education in counteracting the effects of the division of labor.

22. Allen Eaton's *Handicrafts of the Southern Highlands* (New York: Russell Sage Foundation, 1937; New York: Dover, 1973), provides an excellent contemporary survey of the crafts of the Upland South, chronicling the important role played by folk and settlement schools in this craft revival. Two important analyses of the origins of this revival may be found in Henry Shapiro, *Appalachia on Our Mind: The Southern Mountains in the American Consciousness, 1870–1920* (Chapel Hill: University of North Carolina Press, 1978), and in David Whisnant, *All That Is Native and Fine: The Politics of Culture in an American Region* (Chapel Hill: University of North Carolina Press, 1983). Whisnant looks in depth at the cases of the Hindman Settlement School and the John C. Campbell Folk School.

23. The story of ballad collecting and the collectors may be found in Shapiro and in Whisnant, ibid., and in Maud Karpeles, *Cecil Sharp: His Life and Work* (Chicago: University of Chicago Press, 1968), and D. K. Wilgus, *Anglo-American Folksong Scholarship Since 1898* (New Brunswick: Rutgers University Press, 1959).

24. See Shapiro, *Appalachia on Our Mind,* for a discussion of the importance of the role played by mountaineers in providing America with a distinctly Anglo-Saxon "folk."

25. Warren Susman, *Culture as History: The Transformation of American Society in the Twentieth Century* (New York: Pantheon Books, 1984), p. 140.

26. Quoted in Ruth Kedzie Wood, "Henry Ford's Great Gift to the American People," *The Mentor* 17 (June 1929): 1. This entire issue of *The Mentor* is devoted to Henry Ford and his collecting.

27. Michael Wallace, "Visiting the Past: History Museums in the United States," in Susan Porter Benson, Stephen Brier, and Roy Rosenzweig, eds., *Presenting the Past: Essays on History and the Public* (Philadelphia: Temple University Press, 1986), p. 145. Wallace's analysis of Ford is particularly important for its discussion of the ironies of Ford as creator of an idyllic version of the preindustrial past, preserver of particular remnants of preindustrial culture, and as an important force in the development of industrial America.

28. Benjamin Lovett, quoted in "Balance Four-Turn Partners!" *The Mentor* 17 (June 1929): 15.

29. See Eugene W. Metcalf, Jr., "The Politics of the Past in American Folk Art History," in John Michael Vlach and Simon J. Bronner, eds., *Folk Art and Art Worlds* (Ann Arbor: UMI Research Press, 1986); and Eugene W. Metcalf, Jr., and Claudine Weatherford, "Modernism, Edith Halpert, Holger Cahill, and the Fine Art Meaning of American Folk Art" in this volume. For an important critique of the folk art

paradigm, see Kenneth Ames, *Beyond Necessity: Art in the Folk Tradition* (Winterthur, Del.: Winterthur Museum, 1977). For Holger Cahill's commentary on American folk art see Holger Cahill, *American Folk Art: The Art of the Common Man in America, 1750–1900* (New York: Museum of Modern Art, 1932).

30. The Newark Museum Association, *Children at the Textile Exhibition, February 1–March 19, 1916* (Newark: Newark Museum, 1916), pp. 11 and 2.

31. Metcalf compares the concepts of folk art as expressed in the homelands exhibitions with those of Cahill and other collectors in "The Politics of the Past." He also discusses the perspective of Allen Eaton, who played an important role in the organization of these exhibitions under the aegis of the Russell Sage Foundation. Eaton's survey of the homelands exhibitions and philosophy, *Immigrant Gifts to American Life* (New York: Russell Sage Foundation, 1932), is an important primary source. A brief introduction to Eaton's life and work may be found in David B. Van Dommelen's "Allen Eaton: In Quest of Beauty," *American Craft* 45 (June–July 1985): 35–39.

32. Susman, *Culture as History*, pp. 156 and 192–194.

33. Ibid., pp. 171–172; and William Stott, *Documentary Expression and Thirties America* (New York: Oxford University Press, 1973).

34. See Stott, *Documentary Expression and Thirties America*; Pete Daniel, Merry A. Foresta, Maren Stange, and Sally Stern, *Official Images: New Deal Photography* (Washington, D.C.: Smithsonian Institution Press, 1987); and Andrea Fisher, *Let Us Now Praise Famous Women: Women Photographers for the U. S. Government 1925 to 1944* (London and New York: Pandora Press, 1987).

35. Herbert Halpert, "Southern Recording Expedition," 1939, pp. 3–4 Herbert Halpert file, Archive of Folk Culture, Library of Congress, Washington, D.C.

36. William F. McDonald, *Federal Relief Administration and the Arts: The Origins and Administrative History of the Arts Projects of the Works Progress Administration* (Columbus: Ohio State University Press, 1969), pp. 705 and 707; and concerning the Federal Writers' Project, see Jerrold M. Hirsch, "Portrait of America: The Federal Writers' Project in an Intellectual and Cultural Context" (Ph.D. dissertation, University of North Carolina, 1984); and Jerre Mangione, *The Dream and the Deal: The Federal Writers' Project, 1935–1943* (Boston: Little, Brown, 1972).

37. McDonald, *Federal Relief Administration*, p. 711. This was not the case, according to John Michael Vlach, with the Index of American Design. Vlach holds that despite articulated goals, the Index, a collection of 22,000 pictures of significant American objects of folk and popular design, evolved instead into a "shopper's guide" to American antiques. John Michael Vlach, "The Index of American Design: From Reference Tool to Shopper's Guide." (Paper presented to the Annual Meeting of the American Folklore Society, Albuquerque, October, 1987.)

38. R. Serge Denisoff, *Great Day Coming: Folk Music and the American Left* (University of Illinois Press, 1971; Baltimore: Penguin, 1973) pp. 61–62.

39. Denisoff discusses the Highlander Folk School in *Great Day Coming*, pp. 29–31. For more in-depth studies, consult Frank Adams, *Unearthing Seeds of Fire: The Idea of Highlander* (Winston-Salem, N.C.: J. F. Blair, 1975); and John Mathew Glen, "On the Cutting Edge: A History of the Highlander Folk School, 1932–1962" (Ph.D. dissertation, Vanderbilt University, 1985).

40. On Pete Seeger, see David King Dunaway, *How Can I Keep from Singing: Pete Seeger* (New York: McGraw-Hill, 1981); and Pete Seeger and Jo Metcalf Schwartz, ed., *The Incompleat Folksinger* (New York: Simon and Schuster, 1972).

41. See Denisoff, *Great Day Coming*, (1973). Regarding folk song and organized labor itself, Pete Seeger commented that "except for a few unions there never was as much singing as some people now suppose. From listening to the Talking Union record and reading a couple of novels about the labor struggles of the 30's one might jump to the conclusion that the United States was full of class conscious harmonizing in

those days. 'Taint true." Pete Seeger, "Whatever Happened to Singing in the Unions," *Sing Out!* (May 1965): 29, quoted in R. Serge Denisoff, "'Take It Easy, but Take It': The Almanac Singers," *Journal of American Folklore* 83 (1970): 24.

42. Irwin Silber, Notes on *Hootenanny at Carnegie Hall*, Folkways Records FN2512. See Denisoff, *Great Day Coming* pp. 99–121; and Robbie Lieberman, "'My Song Is My Weapon': People's Songs and the Politics of Culture, 1946–49" (Ph.D. dissertation, University of Michigan, 1984) for information about People's Songs, Inc.

43. The source for the discussion of the cowboy hero here is Lonn Taylor, "The Cowboy Hero: An American Myth Examined," in Lonn Taylor and Ingrid Maar, eds., *The American Cowboy* (Washington, D.C.: American Folklife Center, Library of Congress, 1983), pp. 62–176.

44. Bill C. Malone, *Country Music, U.S.A.* (Austin: University of Texas Press, 1985), pp. 141–145.

45. Taylor, "The Cowboy Hero," pp. 134, 140.

46. Ibid., pp. 146–148, 162.

47. Denisoff, *Great Day Coming*, p. 155. For discussion of the commercial folk music revival and the Weavers, see Denisoff, *Great Day Coming*, pp. 136–141 and 154–189.

48. For a relatively contemporary perspective on the meaning of these years, see Charles A. Reich, *The Greening of America* (New York: Random House, 1970).

49. *The Last Whole Earth Catalog* (Menlo Park, Calif.: Portola Institute, 1971), p. 1.

50. Malone, *Country Music, U.S.A.*, p. 281.

51. Toelken, *The Dynamics of Folklore*, p. 23.

Rough Sincerities: William Wells Newell and the Discovery of Folklore in Late-19th Century America

❧ ROGER D. ABRAHAMS ☙

A MERICAN FOLKLORE was an invention of the last generation of the 19th century. Prior to that, the traditional expressions and practices of individual communities or cultures in North America had been noted, but the idea of a larger American tradition or plurality of traditions remained unexplored until the centennial celebration of American independence called for a wholesale examination of the national experience.

This centennial overview of American culture emerged in the midst of a larger examination of national values and practices. The last quarter of the 19th century was marked by a sense that a great accomplishment—profitably populating and domesticating a wilderness continent—was in progress. Counter voices to this hymn in praise of progress sang of lost vigor and pride, and of a diminished sense of the more basic purposes of life that had animated Americans in the past. A good number of intellectuals shared this mistrust of modernity. Like the many European forms of antimodernism, American intellectuals saw a vulgarizing and deinvigorating tendency accompanying "progress." They looked to the past and to an older sense of community and tradition in order to understand their growing sense of alienation and loss.

Concern with the place of tradition in the formation and maintenance of culture led to the founding of groups such as the American Folklore Society, as well as similar organizations. The writers, collectors, public-spirited benefactors, and museum curators who founded the American Folklore Society declared their interest in the body of indigenous expression in the United States that might be collected, scientifically studied, and by this process, woven into the story of the United States. They were bent on recapturing the spirit of the vigorous past by identifying present practices that maintained the "rough sincerities, the hard fights, the hearty loves and hates, the coarse life, the brilliant shows" that characterized how nonlettered peoples organized their lives.[1] They were among the great many thoughtful Americans who had come to feel alienated from a society committed to mechanizing and rationalizing all aspects of life. As counterpoints to this modernism, they idealized earlier epochs (the Middle Ages in particular), simpler societies (such as that of the American Indian), and childhood—all these they saw as times and cultures exhibiting more energy and imagination and encouraging a wider range of vigorous experiences.

When folklore caught the interest of those who came to call themselves folklorists in the 1880s and 1890s, it seemed to be a radical alternative to settled, mechanical, and rationalized lives. While the major current of thought among late-19th century intellectuals was one of rational organization and professionalization, there also was a shared sense that such a stage of civilized activity brought with it a failure to experience life fully. Americans at that time looked back on the Civil War as a time of heroic actions and virtuous motives. They measured their own lives against such a background and often judged themselves harshly as a result. Technology seemed to create habits of mind that undermined the pioneer American zest for heroic endeavor.

Even those not explicitly interested in American folklore as a subject area saw in the frontier experience and the commingling of peoples a way to describe the national character. Both William

James and Henry Adams made numerous comments on common sense and popular notions as a way to study American achievement. Wrote Adams, for instance: "A few customs, more or less local; a few prejudices, more or less popular; a few traits of thought, suggesting habits of mind,—must form the entire material for a study more important than that of politics or economics."[2]

A generation later, Constance Rourke was to attach similar ideas to the study of folklore. Folklore, she noted, seems to arise when social developments have created sufficient distance in time and space that "the folk" come to be considered "delightful," remembered and "read about . . . with a mild nostalgia." Such feelings, she wisely noted, are encouraged when life in the past can be imagined as showing "a coherence lacking in our unstable and heterogeneous social life."[3]

Because the United States was settled by Europeans determined to make a radical departure from Old World ways, Americans were confronted with the question of how to make a culture out of revolutionary motives. Americans and Europeans alike regarded the new nation as a large-scale social experiment that carried promise of cultural renewal. From such a perspective, residues of Old Country customs were noted only as evidence of failure to cast off ignorance and superstition, or as suspicious carry-overs of a religious or class system that the founders of the nation explicitly rejected. It was inconceivable that the folklore of the European past would provide the new nation with traditions that could assert its uniqueness.

There had been a good deal of conjecture about how this new land and this renewing experience might be used as the basis for the formation of new traditions. Emerging first as a consciousness of local and regional characteristics and dialects, a literature of common culture developed that drew upon local resources. Many of the writers in the fledgling republic told local stories in their attempts to build an American sense of tradition. While Washington Irving revised European legends and relocated them in the

Catskills, others wrote specifically American epics, telling the stories of Christopher Columbus or Daniel Boone. Henry Wadsworth Longfellow's epic *Song of Hiawatha*, written at mid-century was, in fact, an imitation of the Finnish national epic, *The Kalevala*, but it drew on the Algonquin myths newly collected and published by Henry Rowe Schoolcraft.[4]

In many ways Longfellow was the key figure for understanding the search for a national culture through regional stories that epitomized the American struggle for identity. His "Courtship of Miles Standish" drew upon the New England past, just as his "Song of Evangeline" told of the Acadians' forced displacement from Quebec to Louisiana. In these poems celebrating the New World through epics of experience, Longfellow presented the most vigorous depiction yet of the American experience to a popular audience. Gathered around the fire, the 19th-century family reading such poems aloud could measure their own comfortable lives against the fancies and hardships of the past.

Not until after the Civil War was there a sufficient sense of national accomplishment to look to the past for more than the heroic stories of the founders. Just as the nation was entering its second century by celebrating the centennial of the American Revolution, there began to arise a realization that there were traditions aplenty to be found throughout the country, enough to warrant the creation of a professional society to collect and publish evidence of such traditions.

A society dedicated to collecting and publishing these evidences might not seem much of an intellectual adventure today, but so it seemed in 1887, when Franz Boas, Francis James Child, and William Wells Newell worked out the first statement of purpose of the American Folklore Society.

At 30, Boas was the youngest of the three. A Berliner and a trained scientist, he had been attracted to the United States through his studies of Northwestern Indian culture. Boas was in many ways the major conceptualizer of the notion of cultural relativism.

Francis James Child, then 63 years old and not in the best of health, was a great scholar of British ballads and the Boylston scholar of Rhetoric at Harvard University. Child's had been a remarkable life. Born into an Irish family in caste-bound Boston, his intellectual abilities were discovered early in his life and he was adopted by the Cambridge intellectual community. At Harvard he took an important part in the development of the new liberal arts curriculum. A strong abolitionist, he was known for his efforts on behalf of the Sanitary Commission and its work to set up a private hospital system for the North during the Civil War. At the time of the founding of the American Folklore Society, Child had already begun publishing his life work, *The English and Scottish Popular Ballads* (1882–1898).

William Wells Newell, at 49, had been a student of Child and had also served with the Sanitary Commission during the Civil War. He shared the older man's passion for medieval life and letters. He found his way to folklore by discovering that some American children's songs and games resembled Child's English and Scottish ballads. Reared in the Cambridge of Longfellow and James Russell Lowell, Newell was a prodigious student who had not yet quite found his promised place in the intellectual life of his community and nation.

These three men—Boas, Child, and Newell—were consciously engaged in a project of cultural intervention. They saw the founding of the American Folklore Society as a moral as well as an intellectual, scientific, and scholarly enterprise. By making the public aware of the rich cultural resources carried by tradition-bearing Americans of all backgrounds, they felt sure that at one and the same time, scientific research might be forwarded, and misconceptions concerning race and culture might be confronted.[5]

An 1894 article on the American Folklore Society by Lee J. Vance recalled the unique features of the society's charter. It emphasized not only the American character of the lore, but the social openness of the founders. "What our folk-lore scholars are 'driving at,'" Vance wrote, is "the importance of the unwritten traditions." Following the conventional rationale for folklore collection, Vance noted the "necessity of gathering the lore of American folk while there are time and opportunity." Unlike earlier approaches that limited folklore to certain isolated cultures, he remarked on the ubiquitous character of the lore: "Every one can add his or her mite, from the farmer to the stock broker, from the servant girl to her mistress." Finally, Vance stated categorically that "the man who is responsible for the very existence of such an organization . . . is William Wells Newell."[6]

While not as well known as Child or Boas, Newell made the greatest contribution in the formation of the discipline of folklore, not only in organizing the American Folklore Society, but in bringing together the various representatives of cultural theory and developing original ideas about how the work of this new discipline might be carried out.

According to the charter statement of the proposed American Folklore Society, published in the first issue of the *Journal of American Folklore*, the society was established "to encourage the collection of the fast-vanishing remains of folk-lore in America,"—not, in other words, to enter into the debates of that day over the origin and dissemination of the world's traditional narratives or ritual systems, and not to use folklore as a way of arguing social evolution—but simply to collect, present, and study folklore in North America.[7]

The very name of the society sounded the message that this society was *not* to be confused with *The* Folklore Society already in existence in England. As Newell was to argue in a number of speeches given over the next decade, English and European folklorists might be wholly devoted to the study of the cultures of the past, but Americans were living in the midst of such lore if they would only recognize it. Just as he had discovered ancient children's games and songs still being played by young Americans of every sort, he argued that folklore entered into everyone's life at some time, no matter how scientific or rational or evolved they might think themselves.[8]

The American character of the new society was spelled out. Collection would be made not only of "relics of Old English Folk-Lore (ballads, tales, superstitions, etc.), " but also of "Lore of Negroes in the Southern States . . . Lore of the Indian Tribes in North America (myths, tales, etc.)"; and the "Lore of French Canada, Mexico, etc."[9]

Given the interest today in ethnic communities in the United States this last "etc." is especially significant. While not spelling out the extent of ethnic groups that should be included in the study of American folklore in his charter statement, Newell later somewhat clarified these matters. "How many nationalities, and in what proportions," Newell exclaimed of American folklore possibilities, pointing especially to how this study will enrich the understanding of town life by having local folklore societies to study the various quarters of a city. He goes on to note the pervasiveness of Germans, Irish, French Bohemians, and Russians, all of whom "bring to our doors the spectacle of the whole civilized and semicivilized world, with its rich development of national costume, customs and superstitutions. . . ."[10] One such local society, the Philadelphia branch, in their chartering statement, called for collection of lore in the various "quarters" of their city or districts, including the lore of roving tinkers, "tramps," and "Sailor's Haunts."[11]

This list not only indicates a pluralistic vision of the American cultures worthy of study; it set an agenda for folklore study in North America that has been followed ever since. But in the 1880s, cultural pluralism was not regarded as a viable model *of* or *for* describing American society. This social pluralistic impulse within the American Folklore Society echoed radical fringe abolitionists, such as Wendell Phillips, who argued an "idea of American Civilization," which was "not a rendering of Protestant, middle-class uniformity" as the historian George Frederickson pointed out, not the "New England writ-large" that it was to most of Phillip's abolitionist contemporaries, but rather a nation made up of peoples of "all races, all customs, all religions, all literature, and all ideas" under the rule of laws "noble, just and equal."[12] Wittingly or unwittingly, the group coming together to form the American Folklore Society resuscitated this older, radical vision of America that had become extremely unfashionable, even among the inheritors of the abolitionist spirit.

Although a number of abolitionists and their children were listed among the founding members of the American Folklore Society, there were also important southerners, such as Charles Colcott Jones, Jr., and Alcee Fortier, both historians and spokesmen for their region. In addition to Child, the first president of the society, and his follower, the great Shakespearean scholar George Lyman Kittredge, there was Thomas Crane, the medievalist, who had been translating and reviewing European folklore studies all his professional life. Almost all the distinguished American historians of the day were members: John Fiske, Francis Parkman, Moses Coit Tyler, and Reuben Gold Thwaites. Philanthropists such as Isabel Hapgood and Mary Hemenway responded to the initial call for membership, as did the great first generation of regional writers: Samuel Clemens, Joel Chandler Harris, and Edward Eggleston.[13] People from a variety of professional backgrounds, such as Oliver Wendell Holmes and the soldier-journalist Thomas Wentworth Higginson, were members as was G. Stanley Hall, one of the founders of American social psychology and the "inventor" of adolescence. Boas had enlisted all the important anthropologists of the day who had been studying American Indian peoples: Horatio Hale, James Mooney, J. Owen Dorsey, Otis T. Mason, Jeremiah Curtin, John Wesley Powell, Alice Cunningham Fletcher, Frank Hamilton Cushing, Daniel Garrison Brinton, Stewart Culin, and Sarah York Stevenson.

The variety of people represented can be understood in part by examining personal connections provided by Newell and his family. Given that Newell and Child were old friends and neighbors in Cambridge, Massachusetts, it comes as no surprise that a great many original subscribers came from that area. Will Newell was the son of Reverend William Newell, who had been the minister of the First Unitarian Church in Cambridge, and the grandson of William Wells, who ran the most influential school in the Boston area throughout the first half of the century. This school numbered among its graduates the literary figures James Russell Lowell, Richard Henry Dana, and Thomas Wentworth Higginson, two of whom became sponsors of the American Folklore Society. Dana, Lowell, and Higginson had all drawn deeply on the materials of folk tradition. Lowell devoted one of his first formal lectures at Harvard to ballads and the problem that he and others of his generation contended with so regularly: how can a new country that has self-consciously cast off the traditions of the old world have a culture, much less a set of oral traditions? Dana wrote of life on the sea, and Higginson recorded the folk expressions of the black regiment with which he served in the Civil War.

Newell graduated second in the Harvard class of 1859 and followed his father into the Unitarian ministry. While the rest of the family gave all the signs of being of a radical social persuasion, Will seems to have been something of a fop. By family report, he dressed in Pre-Raphaelite fashion and dabbled at arts and letters while he pursued the ministry. He served as assistant to Edward Everett Hale, Unitarian minister and author of *Man Without a Country*, and remained his friend throughout his life. Hale also became an original member of the society.

Newell's intellectual interests also influenced the new organization he helped found. A year serving on the Sanitary Commission was followed by his completion of training in theology and several years as a minister, first as an assistant to Reverend Hale, and then with his own congregation, the First Unitarian Church of Germantown, Pennsylvania. Unsuited to this calling, he began a school in New York City that ran for 11 years. He continued to write poetry and began to study medieval literature. Like other self-styled intellectual outsiders of his day, Newell identified strongly with the *trecento*, and saw himself as defending a kind of monastic ideal, albeit an aesthetic rather than a religious formulation.[14]

From his reading of medieval literature and his familiarity with English traditions, Newell discovered, in the world of children's play, still vital traditions that had a long and important unwritten history. His *Games and Songs of American Children* was an historically significant statement in the development of children's culture.[15]

Newell's work on children's lore can be viewed in relation to earlier 19th-century literature that centered on the uniqueness of the childhood experience. Perhaps the first of American childlife works describing the lifeways of an earlier and simpler time was written by S. G. Goodrich in his *Recollections of a Lifetime, or Men and Things I Have Seen*, in 1858. Goodrich was better known in his time as "Peter Parley," the name he used in writing the most influential children's readers of his time. In both readers and memoirs, Goodrich betrayed a romantic vision of childhood and of the American past. Explicitly contradicting those who argued that children are reprobates needing the rule of the rod, Goodrich, like Longfellow, emphasized the relationship between childhood, imagination, and intuitions of freedom and expressions of highly focused capacities to feel deeply. While Goodrich's work did not stress the playful qualities of this childhood world, it did underscore the egalitarian lessons learned in pioneer recreations, such as the bees and frolics of the frontier, in which work was made fun. Goodrich was one of a number of such literary figures who saw life as it was lived in the virtuous "Age of the Homespun" a statement of the relationship between virtue and self-sufficiency, independence and a spirit of sharing in a common enterprise.

In the 1870s a new kind of writing depicted childhood as the time of life valued as a time of its own, a time of comparative freedom, inventiveness, and adventure. The constructive side of play was openly valued, whereas the previous generation had seen childhood as a time in which good work habits should be developed. As Daniel Rodgers has described this change in relation to the stories written about and for children, "the openly didactic work-tied tale," came to be regarded as a relic of the past by the 1870s and a new kind of literature based on actual childhood experiences and the pattern of fairy-tale success stories came into being.[16] This "bad boy" literature is best represented in Mark Twain's adventures concerning Tom Sawyer and Huckleberry Finn.[17]

While Newell was primarily concerned with his discovery that children maintained ancient imitational play in their repertoire of games, his collection suggests strongly that the transmission of this lore went on without the knowledge, much less encouragement, of adults. In league with authors of bad boy literature, then, Newell and his contemporaries viewed children as distinct from adults with a set of beliefs and practices jealously regarded as their own.[18]

The concern at that time with "the childhood of the race," as the evolutionists put it, made such an argument for the singularity of child culture all that more potent. The reigning theory of culture portrayed human accomplishment in terms of the growth of civilization from the stages of savagery and barbarism to simple agricultural societies and finally modern, urban societies. A strong feeling arose that children themselves recapitulated these stages as they grew up, and that they had to experience all of them before reaching maturity.

This stress on childhood as a separate time of life—and on children's culture as distinct from adult culture—can also be seen as a facet of the so-called cult of domesticity and the feminization of American life. Historian Ann Douglas has outlined how motherhood and the practices associated with the home and childrearing provided a language by means of which women assumed power in areas concerned with culture. A loose power alliance between women and ministers to locate the moral center of life in hearth and home, naturally resulted in a higher valuation of childhood and nurturing.[19]

Folklorists, such as Newell and Boas, rejected the rigid and vulgar evolutionism of international folklorists and ethnologists. Newell had discovered among children, as Boas had among the Indians of the Northwest, that folklore was a living phenomenon. Everyone's life was filled with folklore insomuch as each person operates through habit and continues to pass on common-sense information by word of mouth.

Folklorists' interest in both childhood and in earlier, childlike cultures had an impact on the role of women in the American Folklore Society. For women, Darwin's theories of evolution extended to sexual differentiations: women retained more primitive "powers of intuition, of rapid perception, and perhaps of imitation."[20] The American Folklore Society not only saw women as an appropriate subject for folklore studies, but welcomed women among the earliest members of the society. One-tenth of the society's 265 founding members were women; and by the end of the first decade, women accounted for nearly one-third of the membership and participated as officers.[21]

In forming the society, Newell and others were responding to a call to professionalize all intellectual activities, and by implication to raise the status of folklore study and legitimate its pursuit. It is ironic that just at the point when professional independence for folklore might have been declared in the early 1890s, Newell consciously decided *against* making any such claim. Perhaps he did so because most of the membership had already declared a professional allegiance elsewhere. More realistically, Newell had come to rely on the advice of the younger and more energetic Boas, who was busily involved in the formation not only of the American Folklore Society, but also of the Linguistic Society of America and the American Anthropological Association.

Because the 1893 Columbian Exposition (Chicago World's Fair) was to include a number of international congresses, Newell was asked whether the American Folklore Society would organize a congress under the literary section. Boas had already secured Newell's commitment to join in the ethnographic section and argued strongly for continuing that arrangement. The planners of the exposition were annoyed and went to Fletcher Bassett, a Chicagoan whose interests were the folklore and the literature of the sea, and had him organize both an independent local folklore society and an international congress. The Chicago Folklore Society reflected Bassett's literary inclination and the intellectual battle between the anthropologically-oriented American Folklore Society and the Chicago Folklore Society was joined. Few American Folklore Society members attended the meeting, while many European folklorists did.[22] Newell's commitment to the ethnographic section placed the society in a subordinate position to anthropology for the next 75 years.

Newell decided to return to Harvard for a Ph.D. in literature soon after this. He had never relinquished his interest in literature, and he saw his new role that of bringing scientific analysis to the study of Arthurian literature. This was the least successful of his folklore ventures. He did remain editor of the *Journal of American Folklore* well into the 1890s, and he continued to be a leader in the society until his energies deserted him in the middle of the next decade. Although he was eulogized for his immense accomplishment as the founder of the American Folklore Society, it has taken the profession another 75 years to revive his memory and place him in the position of eminence he deserves.

William Wells Newell's vision of folklore as intrinsic to anyone and everyone in this nation of many peoples has provided moral sustenance to all subsequent generations of American folklorists. As his eulogizer, Fred N. Robinson, noted in the pages of the *Journal of American Folklore*, "To him more than to any one else has been due the promotion of the study of folk-lore in America...."[23] To which Boas added: "The strongest appeal to his sympathies lay in the light shed upon the fundamental values of culture by a close study of beliefs, customs, tales and arts of foreign races; in the ability given this study of appreciating the strength and weaknesses of our own culture, and in its tendency to correct the overbearing self-sufficiency of modern civilization."[24]

NOTES

1. The words belong to Charles Eliot Norton, Child's lifelong friend (and Newell's neighbor). They come from his *Notes of Travel and Study in Italy* (Boston, 1859), p. 316.

2. Henry Adams, *History of the United States During the Administration of Thomas Jefferson* vol. 9 (New York, 1889–1891), p. 175.

3. Constance Rourke, "A Note on Folklore," in Van Wyck Brooks, ed., *The Roots of American Culture* (New York: Harcourt Brace, 1942), p. 239. This paper, probably written in the late 1920s, was not published until after Rourke's death in 1941.

4. Henry Rowe Schoolcraft, *Algic Researches: Comprising Inquiries Respecting the Mental Characteristics of the North American Indian: First Series: Indian Tales & Legends* (2 vols., 1839).

5. This was to be Boas's life's work, but was less central to the other two men.

6. Lee J. Vance, "Folklore Study in America," *The Popular Science Monthly* (September 1893): 588, 595.

7. William Wells Newell, "On the Field and Work of a Journal of American Folklore," *Journal of American Folklore* (April-June 1888): 3.

8. Much of my thinking in this area arises from discussions with Michael J. Bell, and from my reading in his "William Wells Newell and the Foundation of American Folklore Scholarship." *Journal of the Folklore Institute* 10 (1973): 7–21.

9. Newell, "On the Field and Work of a Journal of American Folklore," p. 3.

10. W. W. Newell, "Folklore Study and Folk-lore Societies," *Journal of American Folklore* 8 (1895): 237–238.

11. "Hints for the Local Study of Folk-lore in Philadelphia and Vicinity," *Journal of American Folklore* 3 (1890): 78–80.

12. George M. Fredrickson, *The Inner Civil War: Northern Intellectuals and the Crisis of the Union* (New York: Harper Torchbooks 1965), p. 19.

13. Eggleston became an influential popular historian, who cited examples from the folklore and folklife of the American frontier to argue the continuity of European culture, drawing on Francis Parkman's notion of "the transit of civilization." See Robert Allen Skotheim, *American Intellectual Histories and Historians* (Princeton, N. J.: Princeton University, 19), pp. 48–65. In his popular works of history, Eggleston drew upon a great many examples of folk expression; see his *The Transit of Civilization: From England to America in the Seventeenth Century*, 1900; reprinted with a new Introduction by Arthur M. Schlesinger, Sr., Boston: Beacon Press, 1959).

14. Newell was following intellectual fashion in this. The attraction of the age to things medieval is nicely chronicled in T. J. Jackson Lears's *No Place of Grace: Antimodernism and the Transformation of American Culture, 1880–1920* (New York: Pantheon, 1981), pp. 141–182.

15. First published in 1883, and reprinted with additions in 1903.

16. Daniel T. Rodgers, *The Work Ethic in Industrial America, 1850–1920* (Chicago; University of Chicago Press), pp. 125–152.

17. "Bad boy" literature was given its name by Thomas Bailey Aldrich, whose *Story of a Bad Boy* was published in 1869. Another pair of works by Edward Eggleston, *The Hoosier Schoolmaster* (1871) and *The Hoosier Schoolboy* (1883), were also enormously successful, and given to the nostalgic image of growing up as young rascals.

18. Among the founders of the AFS, these collectors included Henry Carrington Bolton, who had written *The Counting-Out Rhymes of Children* (New York: Appleton, 1888); and Stewart Culin, who had included the study of children's games and rhymes among his many antiquarian museum-related interests. See, for instance, his *Games of North American Indians* 24th Annual Report, Bureau of American Ethnology, (Washington, D.C.: Smithsonian Institution, 1907).

19. Ann Douglas, *The Feminization of American Culture* (New York: Knopf, 1979).

20. Charles Darwin, *The Descent of Man and Selection in Relation to Sex* Vol. 3, (1871; Princeton, N. J.: Princeton University Press, 1981), p. 326.

21. Katherine D. Neustadt, "The Nature of Woman and the Development of American Folklore," *Women Studies International Forum*, v. 9, no. 3, (1986): 228.

22. Rosemary Levy Zumwalt, *American Folklore Scholarship; A Dialog of Dissent* (Bloomington: Indiana University Press, 1988).

23. "William Wells Newell," *Journal of American Folklore* 20 (1907): 59.

24. Ibid., p. 63. My thanks to Mike Bell for talking through this argument and to Maggie Kreusi and Janet Anderson for critical readings of the manuscript.

Poor Lo and Dusky Ramona: Scenes from an Album of Indian America

❧ RAYNA GREEN ❧

A young Indian woman with long black hair throws herself over a rough, deep falls.

A handsome, strong warrior with flowing black hair, dressed in buckskins and a full war bonnet, raises his lance and bow to the sky as he sings his death song.

A skulking Indian with a raised tomahawk and scalplock creeps forward from a grove of trees toward a small cabin in a clearing.

An old Indian, his long braids hanging forward over his shoulders, slumps at dusk on a tired pony, his lance dragging on the ground.

A young raven-haired woman, bare to the waist, throws her body over the prostrate and bound figure of a white man. Other Indians, fierce and hostile, loom over them.

THE MAID of the Mist, the Chieftain's Death Song, the Skulking Savage Lo, the Poor Indian at the End of the Trail, and the Tragic Half-Breed or Doomed Between-Two-Worlds Lovers—all figured in scenes from American primal myth in the late 19th century. All were familiar figures by 1900 and continued to be recognizable characters throughout the early part of the 20th century. Particularly in New England and the Middle Atlantic—where Indians had ceased to be common figures in everyday life—romanticized and mythologized representations of Indians were very popular. Plays, poems, songs, local legends, artifacts—all memorialized an Indian gone from the physical landscape. But images and ideas of Indians pervaded so many aspects of life—commercial and recreational—and popular cul-

77

ture that Indians were ever in the forefront of memory and imagination. How did this come to be? How did these particular aspects
of the Indian image come to characterize, even define, American
folk culture and emergent popular culture in the late 19th century?

The heritage of 19th- and 20th-century American romanticism,
to some extent defined by its distinctly Indian "flavor," draws
deeply on European and native-born traditions refined by historical events. European immigrants brought with them folk traditions of belief in the wild man of the forest and the dark
"bogeyman" and the intellectual traditions of "l'enfant sauvage"
and the "natural man." The misnamed "Indian" seemed to fit
neatly into these traditions, and thus became part of the "New
World."[1] The Americas had an Indian identity from the outset.
The earliest iconography representing the Americas was the late
15th- and 16th-century symbol of the Indian Queen. Later the
symbol of America becomes the Indian Princess who eventually
loses her Indianness as she is transformed into the Anglo-Euro-
pean and neoclassic Miss Liberty of the 19th century.[2] The process
of altering a cultural icon so that it conforms to the majority population's notions of itself was coexistent with nationalism and the
development of a national culture.

The original identification of America with Indians, accompanied by embellishment of the primal origin stories through folk
and intellectual traditions, set Indians at the very center of the
American cultural stage. Two contradictory historical facts—the
dramatic and bloodied death and "disappearance" of most Indians
from the American landscape and the growing presence of the
Indian role as an American historical persona—also fixed the Indian image in the cultural repertoire. The juxtaposition of conflicting roles of the Satanic savage and the saintly savior—which both
whites and Indians played as American history unfolded—gradu-
ally created an artistic oeuvre unmatched in popular culture.

During the formative period of American culture—between

1492 and 1700—Indians died of European-introduced disease.[3] In the East, where Indian tribes bore the brunt of the first biological and cultural assaults from Europe, the "disappearance" of Indians was especially dramatic. At the same time, colonial Europeans were struggling to establish a habitat as well as a commercial, political, and cultural presence. They viewed Indians as obstructions to that presence, and thus deemed it necessary to remove them, whether through military and political action or through vigorous and destructive encroachment on all the resources that supported Indian survival. But while colonists felt that Indians had to go, no matter how, the symbolic role of the Indian became essential to Americans. When real Indians could not play the role, other expressive forms had to be developed to subsidize the illusion of an America that was profoundly Indian.[4]

One of the oldest and most pervasive forms of American cultural expression—indeed, one of the oldest forms of affinity with American culture at the national level—is the "performance" of "playing Indian." Since the 15th-century European invasion of North America by the so-called "red hairy men," Europeans found it compelling, satisfying, and useful—indeed, perhaps essential—to play Indian in America, to demand that tribal peoples play Indian, and to export the performances back to Europe (where they thrive even today). The initial forms of playing Indian may indeed constitute some of the "cultural origins of America" in which Europeans were transformed by Indians and Indians were transformed by Europeans into "this new man" hailed by the French immigrant philosopher St. John de Crevecoeur.

Retaining the Indianness of America, without Indians, was a gradual process. Oral tradition, literary tradition, historical event—all had to converge and mix. One of the first strong oral traditions concerned Indian captivities, tales of horror that came to be a popular literary genre, mixing religious and missionary fervor with the American primal scary tale. Of course, for the real captives themselves, becoming Indian was first a necessity; remain-

ing Indian came to be a choice. Echoing many early commentators
such as Benjamin Franklin—indeed, Indians themselves—and
other, later historians, James Axtell states, "The Indians, despite
all odds, succeeded in seducing French and English colonists in
numbers so alarming to European sensibilities that the natives
were conceded to be, in effect, the best cultural missionaries and
educators on the continent." The experience of Indian captivity,
an utterly transforming one, involved the adoption of a tribal
language, as well as of Indian clothes, skills, and mores. Even the
rituals of captivity, quite different from those experienced by Indians in captivity to Europeans, were designed to convert Europeans into Indians.[5]

But European captives took to the role. Other whites, surrounded by Indians, learned to do business and politics Indian-
style out of necessity. Some became so absorbed in dealing with
the Indians that they may even have found it to be enjoyable. For
those who became translators and cultural brokers between the
Indians and other Europeans, it came to be natural, even instinctive. Did they go on hunting trips and war parties with Indians,
learn to walk, stalk game and enemies, and move like Indians? Did
they like the vocalizations—the yells and hollers—and the dances
and songs so necessary to Indian warfare and celebration? Did
they come to enjoy the loosening of European boundaries, the
frisson that comes with acting out a different role? We do know
they took to the role with alacrity and vigor.

Two significant and instructive cultural origin stories about the
first two settlements at Jamestown and Plymouth emerged during
the early 1600s: "Pocahontas Saving Captain John Smith," and
"The First Thanksgiving" or "Squanto Saving The Pilgrims,"
made popular nationally in the late 18th century by the mytholo-
gist Parson Weems, embody the necessary, if somewhat contradictory, components of myths of American national identity. In both
stories, Indians save whites. In the Pocahontas story, an Indian
woman defies her apparently more savage (and in pictorializa-

tions, darker) brothers, father, and friends to "adopt" the military adventurer John Smith. The significance of this event—Smith's ritual death as a white man and his ritual adoption by Pocahontas as an Indian—is lost on Smith in his account of the event and to his faithful fans thereafter. In the other story, the lone Indian, Squanto, befriends the starving Pilgrims and shows them how to plant native crops to survive. The Pilgrims reciprocate by inviting him to the bounteous feast later so memorialized every November. The contradictions in these stories are clear. Squanto becomes Christian; Smith becomes Indian. Other Indians are discarded; whites are saved. "Good" Indians are isolated from their non-deserving compatriots; alone they will eventually perish. Whites, having benefited from the Indians' sacrifice, will take over the Indian roles and memorialize them in some significant way forever.[6]

The Lewis and Clark expeditions shored up American primal myth through tales of the Shoshone Sacajawea, who, like Pocahontas, also saved white men from her fellow savages, and opened up new Indian territories to the invasion of colonists. In the Northeast, where playing Indian had been going on for a long period and thus was more deeply felt, real Indians were almost nonexistent. But westering whites still saw the Indian as an obstruction to their "pursuit of happiness" (read: land). Indian removal, the last barrier to white settlement, and the accompanying reservationization with allotments and leasing of Indian lands, ended finally in the 1880s with the termination of the Indian wars. And the phases and developments in the forms of playing Indian are precisely consonant with those historical periods and consequences. Post-Revolutionary America shifted into westward movement and prosperity, based often on land and land exploitation. Urban eastern America, exemplified by New York, Boston, and Philadelphia, boomed. Indians, in essence, disappear, or get pushed back beyond the boundaries of daily interaction with most Easterners. In the East, Indians are destined to be "loved to death."

Apart from such signal "origin" tales, minor cultural expressions of Indian America began to appear. Little-published books of Indian anecdotes, treaties, and items of linguistic discourse make known the Indian presence in schools and in public oratory since the beginning of the 18th century. Early plays featuring Indian characters such as Pocahontas, Metamora, and Ponteach (Pontiac)—played, naturally, by white actors—began to accustom an audience to the Indian staged presence.[7] In their vaguely eastern Algonkianized costumes—offset with some neoclassic draping—they established a visual style that was later reinforced in cigar-store Indians, figureheads, and the like. The formal staged tableaux were translated for the schoolroom; this way of "playing Indian" became a typical classroom memorialization primarily at Thanksgiving. Songs such as "Alknomook, the Dying Chieftain" were written for underscoring the message that Indians were disappearing.[8] James Fenimore Cooper's works, along with the stage productions and Parson Weems's mythologizing, worked to popularize the idea that there were definite ways to identify "good" Indians and "bad" Indians. They also provided a great sampling of "Indian" vocabulary, which "play Indians" will forever speak: speeches are full of references to chiefs, braves, warriors, princesses, squaws, and papooses. The taste for Indian speeches, authentic or not, became a part of the dramatic repertoire, and "dying Indian speeches" (e.g., Logan's Farewell) joined the songs, the dramatic presentations, costumes, formalized speech, and gestures (facing east or west, raising the arms upward toward the sun) that came to characterize the mythic American Indian—an image that in the 20th century became so familiar in Western movies.[9]

At this point, in the mid- to late-19th century, the developing vocabulary, costume, and other paraphernalia of the performance were refined to a vaguely Algonkianized/Iroquoianized performance. Henry Wadsworth Longfellow's "Hiawatha," written in 1855, helped solidify this image of the Indian. Inspired by the ethnological studies of Henry Rowe Schoolcraft, the Moravian-

Quaker theology of Reverend Heckewelder, and the literary form of the Finnish epic, *Kalevala*, Longfellow offered up Hiawatha, an Algonkianized Iroquois god-hero of the kind found in highly "translated" origin stories and tales. A Hiawatha cult began to thrive not only in America but also in England, where recitations by costumed little girls and boys in school playlets and in Sunday afternoon parlor performances reached its peak. A century of costumed Hiawathas, Minnehahas, and Nokomises speaking of Lake Gitchee-Gumee and Gitche Manito from the stage, spawned jokes, inspired product names, and served as themes for operas.[10]

Popular cultural expression took a new route in the development of Indian themes with the establishment of elaborate Indianized societies. The Tammany Society, with its namesake the legendary Delaware chief Tamanend, emerged in 1789 as a political and fraternal society, supposedly patterned after Indians. Tammany Hall's political corruption in New York City was satirized in 19th-century cartoons. Members were caricatured as chiefs, braves, warriors, and that "old squaw of his" swathed in Indian garb, speaking in mock Indian language and giving war whoops of victory. This visible use of the Indian metaphor transferred to the proliferating social and civic clubs so common to the growth of smaller communities, best later embodied in the Elks, the Lions, the Kiwanis, the Society of Moquis, and so on. The Improved Order of Red Men, with its powwows, victory dances, braves, and princesses, signaled the institutionalization of playing Indian through social organization with its hundreds of chapters; it still persists in regional pockets throughout the continent. All these societies served to introduce the idea of "playing Indian" to the growing middle class, and from the East to the Midwest, which as of the early 1800s was now a part of the United States.[11]

At this juncture in the 19th century, Indian removal begun in the 1830s had reached its peak; the allotment and leasing of land reduced the Indian share to a tiny foothold; the Indian wars of the 1880s depopulated the Indians; and the government had

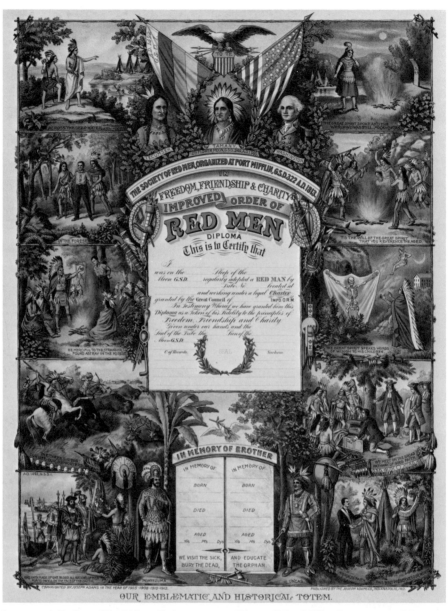

Improved Order of Red Men diploma, 1912. Photo: John Miller Documents. Museum of Our National Heritage.

placed many Indians on reservations or insisted they be assimilated into white society. All these things made real the myth of the Vanishing American. At least for a brief time, it indeed appeared that Indians would go the way of the buffalo, leaving the stage unobstructed for playing Indian. It was the End of the Trail for Indians.[12] Such a myth fed into a burgeoning Indian scholarship. Convinced they must study Indians before they disappeared, scholars would forever be disappointed by Indians that did survive and change.

Scholars looking for a specifically American subject—their own "turf"—to set them apart from their European peers found the "Indian" with later assistance from emergent museums, romantic painting, photography, novels, and dramatic entertainments such as the medicine shows, Wild West Shows, and circuses.[13] Then, Lewis Henry Morgan, with his Iroquois pseudonym (Skenandoah), and his club of would-be archaeologists and anthropologists, began a tradition of would-be Indians that was to continue long into the 20th century, best embodied then by the Zuniesque aspirations of Frank Cushing.[14] At this critical point, too, Morgan drew Iroquois tribal people, such as J.N.B. Hewitt, the Tuscarora scholar, into his Indian club, so that they too, grieved and dispossessed by historical reality, could play Indian as well as the whites who trained them. But Morgan's playacting—composed of singing, drumming, dancing, and oratorical recreating of ceremony—intended to express the depth of his and others' knowledge about true Iroquois culture, in effect, infuriated Indians: it rejected folk and "unscientific" knowledge, regarding as impoverished and increasingly bankrupt the Iroquois store of knowledge and behavior. In essence, Indians became "data," which only objective non-Indian scholars could interpret. And it was these highly selective scholars who often became the key to the storehouse of images, through their writings and museum displays, that Indians and non-Indian alike would draw on for their images. Most significantly, however, American folklore and American anthropology were founded, rooted, and boundaried by the study of—almost an obsession with—American Indians. It was an obsession that served to found most of the large natural history museums in this country—the Field, the Peabody, and the Smithsonian. It was an obsession that inspired the careers of most of the founders of American social science—including Franz Boas and Margaret Mead. The children of Morgan are intimately connected to Indians of the lost past, and the shape of American scholarship, like that of folk and popular culture, is unsurprisingly indebted to the Indianness of it all.

In the last quarter of the 19th century, Wild West shows began to emerge. The last of the old Indian warriors—often Sioux and Crow—were released from military detention to Indian hunters and white Indians like Buffalo Bill to play out the roles set for them. Thus Indians joined whites in playing Indian. The Wild West shows traveled through America and Europe with enormous success. The "warriors," Lords of the Plains—forever mounted on their ponies, forever attacking wagon trains and hunting buffalo— became the archetypal Indian in the American imagination, virtually replacing the Algonkian version.

The author, Karl May—the German counterpart of James Fenimore Cooper—introduced his countrymen to an America he never saw; his tales of Old Shatterhand, the Plains Indian scout, fueled the fires for German versions of playing Indian. Henceforward, then, it was the Plains Indian who was seen as *the* Indian, and the Plains Indian who people played. Perhaps it was no accident that the last and most resilient enemy of Americanization came to symbolize the "typical" Indian.[15]

Like some other well-known Indians, Sarah Winnemucca, the noted Paiute political leader of the late 19th century, found that the Indian role, if played to the satisfaction of whites, offered a chance to carry a political message to a wider audience. Winnemucca, dressed in fanciful garb, became the darling of the reformist movement—which addressed Indian rights as well as tem-

Frank Hamilton Cushing (1857–1900) of the Bureau of American Ethnology dressed
in Zuni attire, 1880s. Photo: John K. Hillers. Cushing was adopted by the Zuni tribe,
made a member of the Macaw clan, and given the sacred name of Medicine Flower.
Photo No. 22-E. Courtesy of the National Anthropological Archives, Smithsonian Institution.

perance and women's suffrage—and began to speak in American lecture halls. As time went on, her clothing became more and more fanciful and she came to be known as "Princess Sarah"—albeit a princess with a strong message for Indian rights. White women who saw her and other Indian "princesses" of the day adopted the same method of social and political commentary, dressed in similar costumes, and performed tableaux in various settings.[16]

These "Indian" performers, almost always dressed as Plains Indians, assumed the characteristics of the stereotypical Indian, speaking in a measured speech, treaty language, and the Hiawathaian methods—using now almost cliches—of "the Great Spirit," "the big water," the "happy hunting ground," and the like, accompanied by raised arm gestures. We see this kind of performance even today: "chief" and "princesses" lead Thanksgiving and Columbus Day parades in full Plains regalia, on horseback; they perform "America the Beautiful" or "The Lord's Prayer" in Indian sign language; they entertain at schools or in social clubs or lodges with "an Indian song" or dance; they stand in front of tourist sites out West (or even some in the East) in full headdress, so tourists can have their pictures taken with them. They serve as the befeathered mascots of football teams, performing mock war whoops and victory dances when the team scores. No matter their specific tribe or affiliation, these Indians are in Plains costume and the gestures and accompanying parts of the act are those of movie Indians. For the most part, they use translated stereotypical names (such as Bright Eyes), which appeal to the non-Indian imagination. A number of Indians earned livings from playing these roles—but many more simply had the goal of supplementing their meager incomes and surviving in the non-Indian world.

The children's game of cowboys and Indians had its roots in the period after the demise of the Wild West show, and was bolstered by Western films. Requiring at most a toy tomahawk and paper feathered headband for the "Indians" (and a cowboy hat and toy gun for the "cowboys"), children's games vitalized the dying forms of playing Indian being abandoned to some extent by the Wild West shows and by the social and civic clubs. The game involves the quintessential cultural roles of brave, squaw, and the like, and draws on a vocabulary of gestures and pidgin-English words. In the fully fleshed-out cowboys and Indians game, the "Indians" "walk Indian file," they howl and yell, putting their flattened palms repeatedly against their pursed mouths in an imitation of the shrill, ritual "lu-lu" of Plains women or the battle cry of men. They greet each other with upraised right forearms, saying "how" (an abasement of the Sioux greeting hau). They stand or sit with arms folded in front of the chest, repeating "ugh!" as a form of communicative discourse. They "creep up" on the cowboys, who, of course, do not engage in such secretive behavior. Here the "cowboys" take on the attitude of British troops accustomed to 17th- and 18th-century European warfare in which soldiers would line up and march straight toward the enemy. The British never quite got over the shock of the Indians' stealthy attacks from the shadows. The Indians are allowed to "run wild," whooping, hollering, behaving in a completely unorthodox manner; the cowboys must behave scrupulously, refusing to "play dirty" and staying taciturn and calm.[17]

The next manifestation of Indian playing was the medicine show. Based on the concept of the Indian as healer, the medicine show borrowed from Indian stage performances, traditional folk repertoire, the Wild West shows, and even circuses. The medicine shows traveled throughout the country offering "Indian" song and dance, and always featuring an Indian selling "medicine" or "snake oil" (usually pure alcohol). Curiously, not only Indians and whites but also blacks "played Indian" in these medicine shows. The medicine shows gave new life to the old drama, as the role of playing Indian became commercially viable and lucrative, signaling to all viewers—European visitors and Americans alike—that the role was worth more than mere attention. While the Indian

Tobacco advertising, ca. 1910; and Wa Hoo Bitters, Old Indian Medicine Company, Toledo, Ohio, ca. 1900. Photo: John Miller Documents. Private collection and Museum of Our National Heritage.

had been a commercial symbol from America's beginnings, as a graphic and sculptural huckster for tobacco products, the medicine show demanded human impersonators as Indian salesmen.[18]

Indians also figured largely in the late-19th century interest in spiritualism. No doubt this was connected with several important notions: that Indians inhabited the spirit world (certainly they had vanished from this one, thanks to the whites), and that Indians

Squaw and papoose tobacco trade sign, 19th century. Courtesy of The Shelburne Museum, Shelburne, Vermont.

Chief Two Moon Bitter Oil advertisement, the Chief Two Moon Laboratory, 1920s. The association of Indians with healing and vitality continued into the 20th century. Photo: John Miller Documents. Museum of Our National Heritage.

were wise and skilled in healing. Thus the spiritualist often claimed to be directed by the guiding spirit of an Indian (this was—and still is—particularly true both in America and in Great Britain). In the accounts of spiritualist practice associated with the Chautauqua movement in New York, in diaries and autobiographies, as well as in interviews with practicing spiritualists, story after story of various chiefs and princesses appear. Interestingly, a century earlier the Shakers had become fascinated with Indian spirits. Late-18th century exponents of the Shaker religion often were "possessed" by Indian spirits in their dances and songs, and would sing in nonsense syllables and make uncharacteristic dance movements. Without doubt, the "Indian" spirit guidance offered yet another way for the Shakers to act outside the rules of conventional behavior.[19]

The Boy Scouts, founded in 1908, added still further to the repertoire of ways to play Indian. Lord Baden-Powell's paramilitary outdoor education movement merged with neo-French revolutionary philosophy, which emphasized the "natural man." The Indian thus came to represent the scouting ideal of manly independence. Learning to walk, stalk, hunt, and survive like an "Indian," to produce beaded and feathered authentic outfits, to dance and sing "authentic" music, to produce tools and weapons—all these skills would become necessary to achieve the Boy Scouts' highest honor, the Order of the Arrow. The scouting reification of the Indian, as Scouts played him (note that by this time the Indian is a definitively male and befeathered Lord of the Plains), allowed more variation than the Indian portrayed by the Wild West and medicine shows. For example, Girl Scouts and Camp Fire Girls (both founded in this century) focused less on paramilitary skill and more on Indian crafts and nature worship in their dramatic reenactments.[20] The Boy Scouts' fixation on Indian singing and dancing created, in its most pervasive manifestation, the hobbyist movement, with its passion for authenticity and perfection in dance movement, in costume.[21] All these themes are perpetuated in summer camping experiences for millions of children even today, and less institutionalized experiences have been memorialized in the writings of Ernest Hemingway and other men-in-nature affiliates.

The turn of the century also saw the advent of tourism from East to West, made possible by trains, and encouraged by the train companies' exploitation of the symbols of the American West.[22] In many ways, tourism to the Southwest expanded the repertoire of Indian folklore from the Algonkianized Eastern images and the

Warriors of the Plains to the Puebloan peoples of the Southwest. Tourists went to the Southwest and saw that Indians had not vanished at all—and moreover, that they were different from the "savages" who populated the Wild West shows. The Puebloan Indians were peaceful and stable peoples who created works of art and held ceremonies. Not only "ordinary" tourists but also scholars, literati, and artists became fascinated with this "new" kind of Indian. Painters, philosophers, and photographers helped generate the myth of the new, western American, a myth fostered by the railroads and the new seekers of El Dorado. It is ironic that the growth of the railroad business—indeed, American business— was tied up with the very people who had stood in the way of expansion and development. And the railroad companies were quick to capitalize on the popular Indian image in their advertisements.[23]

Visits to the American landscape, to the wilderness, and with "natural people" came to be American primal scenes in many ways. Whether people went to Niagara Falls or to the Grand Canyon, they had instinctive feelings of wonder, pride, and affiliation. Similarly, ventures to the American West, having one's picture taken with Navajos or Pueblos, seeing a ceremony of some kind— preferably a Hopi snake dance or a Pueblo rain dance—and acquiring some of the artifacts seen on the journey—a weaving, a pot—were monuments to the visit. Just as Americans used to make the Grand Tour of Europe, now—ordinary and elegant alike— they made the tour of Indian country. The Santa Fe Railway, which named its westbound trains "The Chief," "The Navajo," and "The Super Chief," advertised an American heritage to be acquired with the tour. Their annual calendar, initiated in 1907, was illustrated with works by eastern painters who had migrated— with Mabel Luhan Dodge and others (later Georgia O'Keeffe and Ansel Adams)—to Taos and Santa Fe. Tourists could see this world in slide or magic lantern shows. Calendars, brochures—all advertisements—made the pitch; some even showed Pueblo Indians

For many, part of the tourist experience in the Southwest was to dress in Indian costume and pose with real Indians for the photographer. Dr. and Mrs. Albert Einstein had their pictures taken with Hopi Indians at Hopi House at the Grand Canyon, Arizona, 1931. El Tovar Studio. Neg. 38193. Courtesy of the Museum of New Mexico, Santa Fe.

wearing war bonnets and Plains Indian regalia. Thanks to all these "artworks" and to photography—burgeoning though still in its infancy—every American could have scenes of the Southwest decorating their homes.

Fred Harvey, mogul of the first tourist lodges and trading posts for tourists in the Southwest, joined with the Santa Fe Railway in offering a tourist package called the "Indian Detour." For the first time, tourists could shop at the railway station for Indian pots and Navajo jewelry created by Indians desperate for money in the desperate economy of the teens and 1920s. Harvey and the railway created new markets for these goods, producing as well an enormous curio market—and, in fact, creating the art market for Indian art that exists today. The Atchison, Topeka and Santa Fe Railroad Corporation, in particular, was the "machine in the garden," the technology that made it possible to destroy the natural and native way of life forever; yet it "sold" the image of that life to Americans who still wished to believe in the myth of the ever-expanding West.

By 1920, American popular culture had, in large part, a distinctly Indian cast. The romanticization of the Indian was complete, and that romanticization removed true-to-life Indians from the American consciousness as surely as Andrew Jackson's troops had removed real Indians from the Southwest. Indians had become a symbol of a lost American life and, as such, became an inspiration for ever-renewed American art forms.

> On a football field, a young white man dressed as a Plains war chief dances, whoops, and whirls every time the team (the "Braves" or perhaps "Redskins") makes a touchdown, while the band plays a loud "dum-dum-dum-dum" drumbeat.

> Suburban fathers called "chiefs" and "braves" take their "princess" daughters to Indian craft exhibits and hold "powwows" on the weekends, through the Y-Indian Guides program.

> In an urban neighborhood, a black woman hands out flyers advertising her "reading" service, which features an Indian spirit guide.

> In large, expensive department stores, white women bedecked in turquoise and silver conchos buy designer clothes and shoes styled in the manner of the Old Indian West.

> In a television ad decrying environmental pollution, an Indian—actually an Italian actor playing an Indian—weeps over a garbage-ridden stream.

> In the Black Forest of Germany, large numbers of German families visit their annual summertime "Sioux" encampment, where they spend the week dancing war dances, tanning hides, and taking sweatbaths.[24]

NOTES

1. Many of the lines and phrasings in this essay were printed in my articles on images of the Indian in American culture, references to be found below. I use the term *Indian* because the essay is about stereotypes and images of the aboriginal inhabitants of North America. For treatment of the Indian image in American culture, see Rayna Green, "The Indian in Popular American Culture," in Wilcomb Washburn, ed., *The Handbook of North American Indians, vol. IV* (Washington, D.C.: Smithsonian Institution Press, 1988), for a discussion of images in oral tradition, popular culture, material culture, and classical literature as well as the history of ideas about the "Indian." Also see Robert F. Berkhofer, *The White Man's Indian: Images of the American Indian: From Columbus to the Present* (New York: Knopf, 1978); and Roy Harvey Pearce, *Savagism and Civilization: A Study of the Indian and the American Mind* (Baltimore: Johns Hopkins University Press, 1965).
2. For discussions of the Indian iconography of the New World and the transference from an Indian to a neoclassic image, see Rayna Green, "The Pocahontas Perplex: The Image of the Indian Woman in American Vernacular Culture," *The Massachusetts Review* 16, no. 4 (1976): 698–716; E. McClung Fleming, "The American Image as Indian Princess, 1765–1783; From Indian Princess to Greek Goddess, 1783–1815," *Winterthur Portfolio* 2 (1965): 65–81; and Hugh Honour, *The New Golden Land: European Images of America from the Discovery to the Present Time* (New York: Pantheon, 1975).
3. This figure is generally accepted now by most scholars. At least 90 percent of Coastal Indian peoples in Canada and New England were dead of disease by 1700. See Sherburne F. Cook, "The Significance of Disease in the Extinction of the New England Indians," *Human Biology* 45 (1973): 485–508; Henry F. Dobyns, *Their Number Became Thinned: Native Population Dynamics in Eastern North America* (Knoxville: University of Tennessee Press, 1983). The quantity of primary and secondary literature on contact period America is enormous, as is the amount of literature on specific interactions between native peoples and the British, French, Spanish, and Dutch. The processes of interaction and transformation—of Indians and Europeans—into "Americans" is best described in secondary sources, for example, James Axtell, *The European and the Indian: Essays in the Ethnohistory of Colonial North America* (New York: Oxford University Press, 1981); Neil Salisbury, *Manitou and Providence: Indians, Europeans and the Making of New England, 1500–1643* (New York: Oxford University Press, 1982); Michael Zuckerman, "The Fabrication of Identity in Early America," *William and Mary Quarterly*, 3rd ser., 34 (1977): 183–214; and Francis Jennings, *The Invasion of America: Indians, Colonialism and the Cant of Conquest* (Chapel Hill: University of North Carolina Press, 1975).
4. See Rayna Green, "The Tribe Called Wannabee: Playing Indian in Europe and American," *Folklore* (Spring 1988).
5. For discussion about captives, renegades, and other "white" Indians, see James Axtell, "The White Indians of Colonial America," *William and Mary Quarterly* 32 (January 1975): 55–88; also Colin Calloway "Neither White nor Red: White Renegades on the American Indian Frontier," *Western Historical Quarterly* (January 1986): 43–66; Richard Drinnon, *The White Savage: The Case of John Dunn Hunter* (New York, 1972/1974); and Lewis O. Saum, *The Fur Trader and the Indian* (Seattle: University of Washington, 1975).
6. See Green, "The Pocahontas Perplex," for a complete treatment of the "national" understanding of the tale of Pocahontas; also Philip Young, "The Mother of Us All: Pocahontas Reconsidered," *Kenyon Review* 24 (Summer 1962): 391–415. See Frank DeCaro, "Vanishing the Red Man: Cultural Guilt and Legend Formation," *International Folklore Review* 5 for a provocative treatment of the functions of legends such as the Lover's Leap and other Indian suicide tales. The Rev. Mason Weems, Jr., who

wrote books of instructive tales for schoolchildren of the new nation, was one of the major sources of "national" folklore, including the famous stories of George Washington and the cherry tree, Washington's casting the silver dollar across the Potomac, and others.

7. The very popular anecdote books of the early 19th century put into print much that had circulated in popular and oral tradition in the previous century. Examples are George Turner, *Traits of Indian Character*, 2 vols. (Philadelphia: Key and Biddle, 1836); Pishey Thompson, *Anecdotes of the North American Indian and Natives of the Natural History of the Immediate Neighborhood* (Boston: John Noble, 1857); Harvey Newcomb, *The North American Indian*, 2 vols. (Pittsburgh: Luke Loomis, 1835); and William White, *A Collection of Indian Anecdotes* (Concord, N.H., 1837). See also Richard Moody, "Indian Treaties: The First American Dramas," *Quarterly Journal of Speech* 39 (February 1953): 15–24; and Lawrence Wroth, "The Indian Treaty as Literature," *Yale Review*, n.s., 17 (July 1928): 749–766. The American stage responded to Indians almost immediately, producing plays on these mythic characters, some actually historical, as vehicles for actors like Edwin Forrest (Ponteach). It is interesting to note that one of the most popular dramas, "Ponteach," was written by Major Robert Rogers, a noted Indianized Indian fighter of Roger's Rangers fame. See Arthur H. Quinn, *Representative American Plays from 1767 to the Present Day*, 7th ed. (New York: Appleton-Century-Crofts, 1953).

8. Austin E. Fife and Francesca Redden, "The Pseudo-Indian Folk Songs of the Anglo-American and French Canadian," *Journal of American Folklore* 67, nos. 265 and 266 (July-September, 1954; October-December, 1954): 239–252; 379–454. Of course, the popular stage never quit producing fake Indian songs with fake Indians costumed to sing them, right up through the 1970s with rock-and-roll (e.g.: "Cherokee Woman" and "Half-Breed" by Cher). The ragtime era produced many, the most popular of which were "Tammany" and "The Hiawatha Rag"; see Roger Hankins, "Those Indian Songs," *The Ragtimer* (May–June 1970): 519. Popular stage opera gave us "Rose-Marie," with the famed "Indian Love Call," and country music contributed Hank William's notable "Kaw-Li-Jah," about a wooden Indian who falls in love with another cigar-store maid. The Indian motif, though musically a stereotype unrelated to genuine tribal musical forms, is pervasive in classical and popular American music. See Joseph Hickerson, "A List of Classical American Composers Using Indian Themes" and "A List of American Music With Indian Themes," Archive of Folksong, Library of Congress, Washington, D.C.

9. Such stories appeared first in the popular press, then in tracts. Jefferson made famous the farewell speech of Chief Logan in his *Notes on the State of Virginia* (Paris, 1785), using it to praise both Indian eloquence and prescience, though great debate arose over its authenticity. See Ray H. Sandefur, "Logan's Oration—How Authentic," *Quarterly Journal of Speech* 46 (October 1960): 289–292; also Wilcomb Washburn, "Logan's Speech, 1774," in Daniel Boorstin, ed., *An American Primer* (Chicago: University of Chicago Press, 1966), pp. 6–64; and Ed Seeber, "Critical Views of Logan's Speech," *Journal of American Folklore* 60 (1947): 130–146. Logan's speech, like those of Chief Joseph and Chief Seattle, became staples of schoolroom oration, being reprinted year after year in *McGuffey's Reader*. Benjamin Franklin printed Indian treaties and was fascinated both by treaties as literature and as political thought. Also see Louis Jones, *Aboriginal American Oratory: The Tradition of Eloquence Among the Indians of the United States* (Los Angeles: Southwest Museum, 1965), and Rudolf Kaiser, "A Fifth Gospel, Almost: Chief Seattle's Speech(es): American Origins and European Reception," in Christian F. Feest, ed., *Indians and Europe: An Introductory Collection of Essays*, Edition Herodot Rader Verlag, Aachen, West Germany, 1988.

10. Henry Wadsworth Longfellow, "Hiawatha" (1855); Stith Thompson, "The Indian Legend of Hiawatha," *Publications of the Modern Language Association* (1922); Henry Rowe Schoolcraft, *Algic Researches* (1839); Schoolcraft, *Notes on the Iroquois* (1847);

Rev. John Heckewelder, *Account of the History, Manners and Customs of the Indian Nations Who Once Inhabited Pennsylvania and the Neighboring States* (Philadelphia, 1819). For various treatments of the Indian in American literature and that literature's effect on the European imagination, see Leslie Fiedler, "The Indian in English Literature"; C. Feest, "The Indian in Non-English Literature" in Washburn, ed., 1987, forthcoming; also Leslie Fiedler, *The Return of the Vanishing American* (New York: Stein and Day, 1968); Albert Keiser, *The Indian in American Literature* (New York: Oxford University Press, 1933); Willard Thorpe, "Cooper Beyond America," *New York History* 35 (October 1954): 522–539; W. C. Vanderwerth, *Indian Oratory* (Norman: University of Oklahoma Press, 1971); and Elemire Zolla, *The Writer and the Shaman: A Morphology of the American Indian* (New York: Harcourt Brace Jovanovich, 1973).

11. *Tammany from 1789: The Society of Saint Tammany, or the Columbian Order: Tammany Hall, the Origin and Sway of the Bosses* (New York, 1928). There is little written on the Improved Order of Red Men. I have examined printed materials, handbills, certificates, and ceremonial literature in the collection of the National Museum of American History, the Smithsonian Institution, and the Library of Congress, and I have interviewed former members of an Order chapter in Massachusetts. A very prominent Arizona senator and collector of Indian artifacts belonged to the Moquis during the 1960s and 1970s. The "Moquis" dress up in Indian clothes on ceremonial occasions, and perform "snake" dances and other rites. There is some evidence that more than the name of the very large and important American civic club, Kiwanis, has some Indian roots, but I have not been able to confirm that connection in more than the name, an Algonkianized word.

12. Vivid descriptions of this era can be found in Loring B. Priest, *Uncle Sam's Stepchildren: The Reform of U.S. Indian Policy, 1865–1887* (New Brunswick, N.J.: Rutgers University Press, 1942).

13. The literature on paintings of Indians in the 18th and 19th centuries is abundant. For references, see any works on Charles Bird King, Karl Bodmer, Seth Eastman, or George Catlin for samples of the kinds of paintings mentioned. For photography, see especially works on Edward Curtis.

14. Lewis Henry Morgan (Skenandoah), "Letters on the Iroquois," *American Review* (1847), February 8–18; March 242–256, 447–461; and Curtis Hinsley, *Savages and Scientists: The Smithsonian Institution and the Development of American Anthropology, 1846–1910* (Washington, D.C.: Smithsonian Institution Press, 1981).

15. See Henry B. Sell and Victor Weybright, *Buffalo Bill and the Wild West* (New York: Oxford University Press, 1955), and Don Russell, *A History of the Wild West Show* (Fort Worth: Amon Carter Museum of Art, 1970). For accounts of the European reactions and response to the Wild West show, see Feest, "The Indian in Non-English Literature," especially Daniele Fiorentino and Ulrich Fleisher, "Far West Made in Germany" *Impressionen vom 31, Indian Council in Nidda bei Frankfurt, Country and Western* 6 (Nov.–Dec. 1981): 16–19; see also Arthur Kopit, *Indians* (New York: Hill and Wang, 1969), for a modern literary version of the influence of the genre on American culture.

16. See Joanna Scherer, "The Public Life of Sarah Winnemucca," *Cultural Anthropology* (forthcoming, 1988), for the story of the evolution of Winnemucca's character; see also Dorothy Clarke Wilson, *Bright Eyes: The Story of Suzette LaFlesche* (New York: McGraw-Hill, 1974), for a popularized account of the beautiful and charismatic Omaha sisters, who became the darlings of the reformist movement, further developing the staged personae.

17. I have informally interviewed hundreds of current and former "cowboys and Indians" players throughout the country for their impressions of the game and what it involves. Most say that as children, they fought over who would play which role, most opting for the cowboy role because they did not like "getting beat." Interest-

ingly, those who always opted for the "Indian" role—a group that includes a much higher percentage of women than the cowboy players—are very clear about what attracted them: the costume, the yelling and "acting out" that accompanies the role, and the "underdog" aspects the role entails.

18. The last American medicine show, owned by a black itinerant musician in North Carolina and still featuring "Indian" medicine and performance, closed in the late 1970s. There is not a great deal of published material on the shows; for information about content, one must rely on contemporary news accounts; personal remembrance; and the hundreds of medicine show posters, flyers, photographs, handbills, and the like in museum and archival collections at the New York Public Library, the Smithsonian Institution, and the Library of Congress. See Arrell Gibson, "Medicine Show," *The American West* 4, no. 1 (February 1967): 34–39, and Brooks McNamara, "The Indian Medicine Show," *Education Theatre Journal* (Dec. 23, 1971):431–449. So-called Indian doctor products sold by the shows were followed by "Quaker" and "Shaker" doctor products.

19. Little literature exists on the Indian guide phenomenon per se. I and my students have interviewed black and white spiritualists in New York, Massachusetts, and Washington, D.C. I have a small collection of reader/palmist/spiritual guide handbills from black spiritualists in Washington, all of which are mass-produced with the names of individual spiritualists inserted into the boilerplate. All feature an Indian with headdress as a logo and the designation of "Indian guide" given to the particular "reader's" directing influence. Only recently in England, I heard of the White Eagle Lodge, guided of course, by Chief White Eagle. For Shaker songs, see Edward D. Andrews, *The Gift to be Simple: Songs, Dances and Rituals of the American Shakers* (New York: Dover, 1962).

20. See Charles Alexander Eastman, *Indian Scout Talks: A Guide for Boy Scouts and the Camp Fire Girls* (Boston: Little, Brown, 1914) for an Indianized inspiration for playing Indian to the scouts. See also Boy Scouts of America, *A Handbook for Boys* (New York: Grossett and Dunlap, annually produced by the Boy Scouts of America); see also the European and international versions of the manual, as well as manuals for the Camp Fire Girls and the Girl Scouts of America.

21. William Powers, "The Indian Hobbyist in America"; Colin Taylor, "The Indian Hobbyist in Europe"; and for movies, Michael Marsden, "The Indian in Movies," all in Washburn, *The Handbook of North American Indians*, 1988.

22. See Lois Palken Rudnick, *Mabel Dodge Luhan: New Woman, New Worlds* (Albuquerque: University of New Mexico Press, 1981), and Arrel M. Gibson, *The Santa Fe and Taos Colonies: Age of the Muse, 1900–1942* (Norman: University of Oklahoma Press, 1983).

23. T. C. McLuhan, *Dream Tracks: The Railroad and the American Indian, 1890–1930* (New York: Abrams, 1985).

24. For references on contemporary manifestations of the Indian images, see "Plastic Medicine Men," (Summer 1987); "Record of Councils Held by the Traditional Circle of Elders," *Akwesasne Notes*, (Fall 1987): 4–6; Feest, "The Indian in Non-English Literature," pp. 309–329; also Stewart Brand, "The Counter Culture and Indians, 1960s–1970s," in Washburn, "Happy Hippie Hunting Ground" and "Return of the Red Man," *Life Magazine* (December 1, 1967); "The Indian Ordeal," *New York Times Magazine* (1987). On the Y Indian Guides, I have derived my description of the program from several accounts in the *Washington Post* (1986 and 1987) and from several telephone calls to the American Indian program office by "chiefs" wanting to arrange museum tours of Indian exhibits for themselves and their "princesses." See Green for a slightly more extended commentary on sports play; also "Indians Open War on Redskins" and "Redskins Keep Name, Will Change Lyrics," both in the *Washington Post* July 15, 1972, p. D-1, and March 30, 1972, p. A-1; also Ralph Linton, "Totemism and the American Air Force," *American Anthropologist* 26 (1920): 296–330. For modern European phenomena, see Feest, "The Indian in Non-English

Literature," pp. 309–328; Peter Bolz, "Life Among the Hunkpapas': A Case Study of German Indian Lore," pp. 475–490; Rudolf Conrad, Rudolf Kaiser, Miklos Letay, and Giorgio Mariani; "Was Anybody More of an Indian than Karl Marx? The 'Indiani Metropolitani' and the 1977 Movement," pp. 585–598; Alexander Vaschenko, "Some Russian Responses to North American Indian Cultures," pp. 307–320; Christopher Mulvey and Ewa Nowicka, "The Polish Movement Friends of the American Indians," pp. 599–608. For literary romanticism, see Carlos Casteneda, *The Teachings of Don Juan: A Yaqui Way of Knowledge* (New York: Simon and Schuster, 1969), and succeeding volumes, *A Separate Reality: Further Conversations with Don Juan* (1971), *Journey to Ixtlan* (1972), and *Tales of Power* (1974), Lynn Andrews, *Medicine Woman* (New York: Harper & Row, 1981), and *Spirit Woman*, and *Jaguar Woman*, succeeding years.

Packaging the Folk: Tradition and Amnesia in American Advertising, 1880–1940

❧ JACKSON LEARS *☙*

O NCE UPON A TIME, there was a place called traditional society. People lived on farms or in villages, at one with nature and each other. For these preindustrial folk, there was no separation between the home and the world, between labor and the rest of life. They worked hard but their lives were unhurried, governed by the rhythms of the seasons rather than by the ticking of the clock, endowed with larger purpose by a supernatural framework of meaning. They passed the time, rather than saving it or spending it, in easy sociability with people like themselves. Together they constituted a static, homogeneous social group, rooted in the soil and in face-to-face relationships. But the urban-industrial transformation brought an end to this organic community. Religious beliefs eroded, social bonds stretched, class antagonisms formed and sharpened. People escaped the drudgery of the farm only to find themselves huddling in fetid, anonymous streets, scurrying to routine jobs in factories and offices. Through the brown fog of a winter dawn, they glimpsed the rise of modern society.

That is the story social theorists have told themselves for over a century, in a variety of idioms. Those following the lead of the German sociologists Ferdinand Tönnies and Max Weber have stressed the importance of secularization in dissolving the ties that bound the folk in the organic community; for them the transition from folk life to modern life has been a linear, irreversible process—tinged with sadness, perhaps, but somehow inevitable. Thinkers in the Marxist tradition, while celebrating ascent from what the *Communist Manifesto* called "the idiocy of rural life," have nonetheless emphasized the exploitative relationship that has developed between town and country, the tendency for urban capital to reduce the countryside to colonial status, using it as a reservoir of cheap labor and raw materials. Whatever the nuances of interpretation, most theorists have used a bipolar framework to characterize the great transition—from *Gemeinschaft* (community) to *Gesellschaft* (society), from feudal to bourgeois society, from tradition to modernity.[1]

In recent years the bipolar model has drawn fire from two directions. Some critics have shown how communal folkways have survived in city settings; others have argued that "traditional" societies were just as fragmented, mobile, and secular as modern societies supposedly have been. Among historians and social scientists, the notion of an organic community is now dismissed as little more than a convenient methodological fiction. *Gemeinschaft* is something the historian declares existed just before the period he or she has chosen to study, when its disintegration provokes the "search for order" that animates his or her subjects. An attitude of skeptical dismissal toward any notion of folk community is especially appealing to American historians, chroniclers of a nation without a feudal past, where (if Carl Degler can be believed) "capitalism came in the first ships."[2]

Yet both within and outside the academy, belief in an American folk has persisted. Given the resilience of that belief, we might consider taking it seriously rather than merely dismissing it as a nostalgic myth. It is probably pointless to try to locate an organic community in a specific place and time; the most important *gemeinschaft* may well have existed in people's minds. So it might make sense to examine the imagery of preindustrial life in industrializing America, attempt to disclose its sources and significance, see how it has served particular needs and interests under specific historical circumstances. The implications of this inquiry are far-reaching: it raises the question of how popular conceptions of the past are formed, outside the precincts of professional historiography; it suggests the complex role of commercial imagery in constructing (and deconstructing) a kind of collective memory; it asks, in the end, whether one can even speak of collective memory in a society whose rulers systematically erase the past and dedicate themselves to the promotion of endless "growth."[3]

We are most familiar with the image of a static, homogeneous "folk society" propounded in the work of Robert Redfield and others in the mainstream of American social thought.[4] The rhetoric and iconography of advertising offer us some more frankly commercial versions of that imagery. Depending on the historical moment (and the advertiser's particular purpose), advertising could represent folklife as an endless round of drudgery or a bucolic idyll; the male folk could be virtuous husbandmen, ignorant rubes, or "progressive farmers"; the women could be grandmotherly sources of wisdom or bent-backed beasts of burden. The contradictions embody confusions in the minds of the people who created the images—people who had left the "folk society" (if they had ever known it) and entered the urban "chromo civilization," but who preserved some ambivalent attraction to folklife. Ultimately, commercial representations of the folk could be as laden with irony as their academic counterparts: in both instances, modernizing institutions (the research university, the modern corporation) could create a sentimental vision of the folkways they had helped to shunt aside, to render irrelevant.

To begin understanding the packaging of the folk, we need to keep certain universal experiences in mind. All people, even academics and advertisers, once were children; many may have experienced a sense of pain and loss en route to adulthood—the "separation anxiety" that Rodney Olsen has argued was particularly resonant in market society, where the establishment of adult identity required the severing of family ties and (often) the uprooting of the individual from familiar surroundings.[5] Many urban professionals, the sort of people who fashioned theories or advertisements for a living, may have associated memories of wholeness with a childhood spent in a rural or village setting. People in and out of the academy sought some linguistic formula to capture their own sense that an abyss of feeling and experience had opened between the industrial present and the preindustrial past. In many lives, dislocating historical changes combined with the universal experience of growing up to shape representations of a preindustrial "world we have lost." It is not fortuitous, in other words, that the word *nostalgia* originally meant "homesickness."[6]

At the same time, certain Protestant traditions gave particular impetus to belief in a virtuous folk. Pietist sentiment elevated faith over works, authenticity of spiritual experience over the artifice of outward observance. The plainspoken *gude-man*, the man of simple words and steady habits, became a cultural ideal set over against the luxurious and deceitful fop. From William Bradford on, Puritan leaders sought to maintain a righteous community based on plain speech and plain living, amid the temptations of a modernizing commercial society. The tension between virtue and commerce became explicitly political during the Revolutionary era, when orators presented the colonists as a band of sturdy republican producers, seeking to preserve their "publique good" and their economic independence from the parasitical claims of imperial bureaucrats.[7]

As the Revolutionary generation passed from the scene, republican contrarieties entered public discourse. The yeoman farmer and the independent artisan stood at the moral apex of a producer ideology. It counterpoised the virtuous folk—who created wealth through their own labor—with the conniving merchants and middlemen—who merely preyed on the labor of others. The producers' leather aprons and muddy overalls were emblems of their authenticity; they did not need to conceal their character behind elegant dress or phrases. They spoke and lived plainly. The key to value in this ideology was economic independence, rooted in the ownership of land or craft skills. The persistence of household production—or the ideal of it—promoted the domestication of republican ideals. As long as work and home remained together, on the farm or in the domestic workshop, public and private virtue could be merged. The merger was more problematic in cities or factory towns. Nineteenth-century producer ideology tended to locate the virtuous folk on farms or in villages.[8]

The producer ideology was narrow in many ways—xenophobic, patriarchal. And its sharp opposition between virtue and commerce tended to obscure the commercial ambitions of the producers themselves. But it had this strength: it took power relationships into account. From the artisans who followed Tom Paine in the 1790s to the Populists of the 1890s, producer ideologues insisted that the relationship between folk virtue and urban commerce was political. In this they resembled Marxist thinkers: they recognized that the great transformation they were witnessing in the 19th century was not simply a neutral, inevitable historical process—a "modernization." Rather, it involved the reduction of some classes of people to dependence on others: artisans on factory owners, farmers on railroad entrepreneurs and commodity traders. The ideal of an independent American folk energized political discourse throughout the 19th century; however confused or sticky with sentiment, it represented a protest against the encroachment of a national market into ordinary people's lives.

The republican tradition was an important source of folk imagery, but by the late-19th century a more pervasive and enduring one had arisen: the apparatus of commercial distribution, which was displacing preindustrial folkways while it celebrated their charm. During the decades following the Civil War, entrepreneurs developed a mass market in images. From Currier & Ives prints, advertising trade cards, and other ventures in chromolithography, we can piece together the fragments of an incipient "media culture." It shared many themes with popular fiction as well as with other emergent forms of mass entertainment.[9] The vision of folk-life embodied in this early media culture tended to be celebratory, though sometimes the celebration contained a modernizing agenda. As control of the traffic in images (and commodities) began to shift from regional entrepreneurs to national corporations, the latent hostility between town and country became more overt. An unambiguous enthusiasm for urban sophistication gained the upper hand by the teens and 1920s. Yet the appeal of folklife never disappeared, and folk images resurfaced during the Depression years, when advertisers' confidence in their own vision of modernity wavered as never before.

To the 1890s, trade cards represented folklife as an idyll passed amid icons of abundance and American nationality: apple-cheeked babes cavorting about shocks of wheat; lovers sighing alongside babbling brooks; Ceres bestriding the globe in stars and stripes. Advertising for a variety of products—parlor organs, root beer, candy, cereals, coffee, dry goods—exalted the prosperous yeoman, his fecund wife, and their cherubic children. The imagery closely paralleled much that was available in Currier & Ives prints or the work of "fine" artists such as Winslow Homer.[10]

The celebratory mood was especially apparent in advertising for agricultural implements and supplies, which often played on republican mythology. Wooldridge Fertilizer quoted George Washington in 1891: "Agriculture is the most healthful, the most useful, and the most noble employment of man," and three years later the McCormick Company saluted the farmer as "our country's defender, the builder of our national prosperity, and the Guaranty of our future greatness."[11] Republican pastoralism combined with emblems of natural abundance to domesticate technological innovation, as threshers and harvesters were surrounded by bare-breasted goddesses, buxom fruits, and tumescent vegetables. Machines, like money in the classical Marxist formulation, were accorded magical powers of increase when allowed to penetrate the fertile womb of Mother Earth. The promise

The Cereals Manufacturing Company trade card, ca. 1890. Courtesy of the Collection of Advertising History, Archives Center, National Museum of American History, Smithsonian Institution.

of abundance required a program of technological development, but the iconography of mechanization was pastoral, and even mythological.[12]

Pastoralism abounded, too, in advertisements for patent medicines—the earliest and most successful nationally advertised commodity. Enthusiasm for the folk was if anything even more intense in this field than in agricultural advertising. Patent medicine manufacturers sought to link their products with the supposed good health of the American countryside and also with the vitality offered by more exotic folk: Amerindians, Peruvian aborigines, shamans from southern Africa. Advertisers paraded the alleged tribal origins of their goods, offering a primitivist critique of American "overcivilization." "It would almost seem," a pamphlet for Dr. Green's Nervura asserted in 1887, "that nervousness, nervous weakness, and prostration had become the national disease, to such an extent have afflictions of this nature increased during the last five years." All neurasthenics could profit from Dr. Green's Nervura, which was made from "a wonderful tropical plant . . .

Cover, McCormick Reaper Company catalogue, 1894. Courtesy of the Collection of Advertising History, Archives Center, National Museum of American History, Smithsonian Institution.

almost worshiped for its curative powers."[13] Primitivism was rooted in popular distrust of doctors' pretensions to expertise—a distrust that was well founded, given the abysmal quality of mainstream therapeutics during the entire 19th century. Only after the perfecting of diphtheria antitoxin in 1894 could the allopathic medical establishment begin to consolidate much cultural authority; before that time it was merely one of many contentious rivals for public support. Small wonder that many a patent medicine presented itself as "the people's remedy"—a democratic alternative to expensive, dangerous, or inaccessible professional care. Until the Pure Food and Drug Act of 1906 (and even to a certain extent afterward), patent medicine manufacturers cried their wares as authentic folk medicines, and decorated their literature with pastoral or primitivist imagery.[14]

Yet even though advertisers praised the wisdom and vigor of the folk, the fact remains that trade cards and catalogues were artifacts generated by an emerging national market—a system of exchange increasingly dominated by large corporations, that posed fundamental challenges to indigenous rural ways: celebrating urban amusements, urging scientifically managed agriculture, mandating dependence on "expert" elites. So it should come as no surprise that besides paying saccharine tribute to rural ways, commercial imagery sometimes ironically bracketed evocations of farm life, as in the N. C. Thompson Company's "Pleasures of Farm Life" series. The "pleasures" included "ye sprightly bumble bees," "ye pesky boys," and "ye borrowing neighbor."[15] Nor is it startling that there was a great deal of rube-in-the-big-city satire in late-19th century advertisements, particularly those directed at urban audiences. From the city point of view, the sturdy yeoman could be just another hick.

Outside the symbolic universe of advertising, urban-rural conflict was more direct. It intertwined economic interest and cultural values. Rural hostility to railroads, for example, was more than a matter of unfair freight rates. The railroads brought with them

"The Maiden Reaper," McCormick Harvesting Machine Company trade card, 1885.
Courtesy of the Collection of Advertising History, Archives Center, National Museum
of American History, Smithsonian Institution.

the institutions of urban consumer culture, particularly the saloon, which was typically a franchise operated by one of the major breweries. In rural Protestant eyes, the saloon epitomized the intrusive, disruptive powers of the national corporate market.[16]

The same sort of tensions emerged in the realm of advertising and publicity. The advertising trade press jeered at country editors' distrust of "foreign [i.e., national] advertising" in their papers, and condemned "the substitution evil"—the tendency of small-town merchants to substitute local for national brand-name products. Long-standing rural distrust of peddlers could easily extend to drummers, national advertisers, and other representatives of the national market; like the peddlers, they lacked local ties and accountability. Country store owners had obvious financial incentives to resist the inroads of corporate advertisers, chain stores, and mail-order catalogues—all institutional embodiments of the encroaching national market. Sometimes the rural population supported this resistance; sometimes local merchants could provoke as much hostility as their rivals in Chicago or Kansas City. The patterns of urban-rural conflict varied according to specific circumstances. There was never any simple confrontation between rural tradition and urban modernity. By the late 19th century, American farmers were too enmeshed in commercial networks to be characterized as self-sufficient producers. Nevertheless, the city-country polarity was genuine and deep. In the rhetoric of country editors and national advertisers, a conflict between two kinds of commerce became a war between two ways of life.[17]

The struggle for legitimacy intensified as major corporations tightened their control over commercial imagery. In attempting to reach a sprawling mass of consumers, national advertisers increasingly employed the services of advertising agencies. The rise of these agencies reinforced the development of the modern corporation as the central force in the shaping of American cultural life. Before, the commercial assault on rural ways had been piecemeal; now it was systematic. Advertisers conceived themselves to be a modernizing, standardizing elite—promoting slick urban styles and modern conveniences, spreading the gospel of "go-ahead" and pep. Agency staff members—from senior account

Cover of Warner's Safe Remedy Company Almanac, 1883. Courtesy of the Collection of Advertising History, Archives Center, National Museum of American History, Smithsonian Institution.

executives to cub copywriters—were on the whole educated and affluent WASP males. After the turn of the century, they tended increasingly to have Ivy League degrees and prejudices. They were metropolitan, secular, "smart," and insulated from the common life of the country. As employees of large bureaucratic organizations who manipulated symbols rather than making things, they had much in common with the emergent "new class" of salaried managers and technicians—in particular a faith in the developing hegemony of professional expertise. In part, for advertisers at least, this was making a virtue of necessity. After the Pure Food and Drug Act of 1906, for example, most patent medicine advertisers realized they had to make their peace with the consolidated authority of the medical establishment. Advertisers had a more general problem as well: they needed to shed their Barnumesque inheritance and establish the legitimacy of their "profession." That accounted for the constant straining after "sincerity" in the trade press, and the many contorted strivings for "truth in advertising" during the early years of the 20th century. But despite the temptation to dismiss advertising professionalism as a mere tactical ploy to avoid government regulation, there is no doubt that advertisers shared a fundamental conviction with other professionalizing elites: a belief in the incapacity of ordinary citizens to manage their affairs without the advice of people like themselves.[18]

By the teens and 1920s, that prejudice was receiving social science sanction in proliferating theories of crowd psychology and mass behavior. For advertisers as well as for other educated and affluent Americans, the notion of a "mass man" with a "14-year-old mind" acquired statistical confirmation in the Army intelligence tests administered during World War I. What was emerging in the trade press was an image of "man" (and even more surely of "woman") as a frivolous and dependent creature.[19] The assumption that "the complexity of modern life" could not be negotiated without dependence on professional expertise posed a decisive challenge to the republican ideal of the independent producer-citizen.

National advertisers muted that challenge by creating the image of the "progressive" consumer—the person who acknowledged his dependence on corporations and sought the advice of experts (particular advertisers). As an in-house handbook published by a leading agency put it in 1909:

> Advertising is *revolutionary*. Its tendency is to overturn preconceived notions, to set new ideas spinning through the reader's brain, to induce something that they [sic] never did before. It is a form of progress, and it *interests only progressive people*. That's why it thrives in America as in no land under the sun. Stupid people are not much impressed by advertising. They move in a rut of tradition.[20]

The antithesis between smart moderns and stupid traditionalists was particularly sharp in advertising directed at farmers. As early as 1880, J. Walter Thompson (who founded the agency bearing his name in 1864) wrote that "the farming community of our country is divided into two classes—one a shiftless ne'er-do-well, the other the bright sharp shrewd and intelligent man, who is wide awake to his own interests and who constitutes in his personality the backbone of our country."[21] The latter was the advertisers' target; he could be counted on to heed their messages. By 1908, the trade press was announcing that many farmers had transformed themselves from hayseeds to "test-tube farmers" who were as likely as their city cousins to drive a "benzine buggy" and wear stylish "collegian" clothes. The rural folk, in other words, could be admired to the extent that they shed their peculiar folkways and adopted the "progressive" world view of national advertisers.[22]

The rhetorical elevation of the "progressive" farmer had wide-ranging cultural implications. At about the same time the ideology of national advertising was slipping into high gear, the commercial iconography of rural life was radically transformed. One could say it reflected a broader disenchantment with the world: after 1900, Ceres and other mythic emblems of abundance disappeared;

fanciful chromolithographs gave way to black-and-white photographs showing the latest tractor or cream separator in action. Like other national advertisers, especially those with machinery to vend, farm implement companies embraced photography for the feel of "real life" they believed it imparted to their goods; in actuality they were exchanging one set of aesthetic conventions, rooted in mythological imagery, for a new set, based on the fiction that through photographic technique the advertiser could provide an absolutely transparent window on the world. But the consequences of disenchantment were political as well as aesthetic. In collapsing the old republican distinctions between virtue and commerce, independence and dependence, farm and factory, the new strategy depoliticized the imagery of the agrarian folk. As early as 1891, while Populist protest was nearing its height, an almanac distributed by the Wooldridge Fertilizer Company illustrated the process by constructing this anecdote: at a Farmers' Alliance meeting in Virginia the speaker fails to show up; a Wooldridge salesman fills in and gives a rousing speech on behalf of fertilizer as the solution to all economic problems. "Away with political parties! Orchilla guano is the key to independence!" he concludes.[23] This miniature melodrama was emblematic of a broader rhetorical pattern that would develop with particular clarity in the years after the turn of the century: the substitution of technical for political solutions to farmers' problems.

After 1900, more and more national advertisments clearly exalted technique to their affluent urban audience, thus devaluating customary ways. The selling of packaged food products is a clear example. Throughout much of the 19th century, urban food retailers routinely watered their milk, colored their cheese with red lead, and extended their coffee with sawdust. A business adage held that "adulteration is just another form of competition." By comparison to the adulterated products of urban chicanery, food on the farm preserved an aura of authenticity.[24] But beginning around the turn of the century, national advertisers presented a third way, with "scientific" guarantees of purity. A 1904 advertisement for Nabisco, for example, presented two Dickensian codgers in frock coats, carrying canes. The caption read:

> Times and clothes have changed, and so have soda crackers. And yet a few people, as a matter of habit, still buy soda crackers in paper bags, which in their way are as old-fashioned as the clothes of our ancestors.
>
> Progressive people—thinking people—have with their manner of dress, changed their manner of living. Instead of buying food in *the open*, they prefer that which has been protected from dust and other things neither pleasant to the palate nor wholesome for the body.
>
> Thus they buy Uneeda biscuit, the finest soda cracker the world has ever known, in an air tight moisture proof package, which ensures beyond question the freshness and goodness of the contents—the price being only five cents.[25]

The cracker barrel, that emblem of rural sociability, was rejected in the name of standardization and sterility. The coffee bin met the same fate.[26]

The attack on rural foodways undermined entrenched sentiments. Even Grandmother had to be dethroned from the seat of culinary wisdom. National advertisers joined the ranks of nutritionists in urging housewives to abandon the heavy, rich meals that Grandma used to make, down on the farm. They packaged foods as the salvation of the inexperienced cook and a marvel to Grandma herself. "GRANDMOTHER AMAZED AT FRUIT-CAKE MADE IN TWO MINUTES" was the headline in a Dromedary Dixie-Mix advertisement of 1934; it summarized four decades of advertising for corporate food processors, who assumed a stance of pragmatic efficiency against the sweet but superannuated traditions of the country kitchen.[27]

What was happening here was not so much the rejection of old, mythic ways of thinking as it was the construction of new myths on the ruins of the old. The great trick was to turn standardization, sterility, and hyper-rationality into the stuff of mythic fantasy. The nearly self-parodic language of extremes ("the finest soda cracker the world has ever known"), the obession with purifying the self and its environment, the epic struggle of the godlike hero-scientists against monstrous yet mysteriously invisible enemies—there was more than simply "rationality" in these features of the emerging rhetoric and iconography. They were key elements in the developing mythology of corporate-sponsored scientific progress.

Yet the mythic dimensions in the advertisers' rhetoric were concealed (even from the advertisers themselves) by their own aesthetic conventions—particularly their literalist assumption that they could provide an unproblematic representation of reality. From the advertisers' point of view, the modernization of diet simply required the consumer to face facts. Many adopted the stance of truthtellers ripping the veils of sentiment off the rural past. An advertisement for Meadow Gold Butter in 1909, promising "Better Butter Than Country Butter," summarized the case against rural foodways: "When you take the sentiment away from 'country' and 'farm' butter all you have left is just plain butter, some good, some not so good. The real facts are that Meadow Gold Butter, churned in our modern sanitary creamery . . . is made under more healthful conditions and is better butter in every way. . . . " The mythology of scientific progress allowed advertisers to wrap themselves in "real facts" and reverse the ancient rhetorical pattern of rural purity and urban corruption. The "modern, sanitary" modes of mass production promised escape from the dirt and disorder of the countryside.[28]

Other rural practices were more easily devalued. Farm life had always required hard work, and for women the toil could be unremitting. Beginning in the 1890s, appliance and laundry product manufacturers presented their wares as a means of liberation from the endless round of preindustrial drudgery, an entree into a world of leisure and self-cultivation. "Wash board or key board? Which has the most [sic] charms for you?" Central City Soap asked in 1904.[29] This promise of leisure became an enduring theme throughout the 20th century; Dromedary's "fruitcake baked in two minutes" was another among many examples of advertisers' assumption that all household work was degrading and ought to be kept to a minimum.

Given our culture's continuing fascination with "labor-saving devices," the problems with this assumption are not immediately apparent. Nevertheless, they do exist. The first is related less to the assumption than to its consequences, or lack of them. Ruth Schwartz Cowan and other historians have pointed out how advances in household technology, designed by men, have actually created "more work for mother" as pseudo-scientific standards are imposed on household work.[30] The second problem is more fundamental: it involves advertisers' tendency to reduce all household work—cooking and childrearing as well as cleaning—to the same plodding level, no matter how much care or craft might be involved. In the symbolic universe of advertising, there was at least a rhetorical devaluation of household craft skills that paralleled the degradation of labor in the early-20th century factory.[31]

Besides dismissing housework as a pointless waste of valuable time, advertisers presented it as a threat to youth, health, and beauty. In 1919 the makers of Joy detergent warned that "rubbing and scrubbing . . . is what makes a woman look old and have rheumatism," as they pictured a bar of soap washing windows while a happy woman watched.[32] Here and elsewhere, advertisements implied that the commodity possessed magical powers to arrest the process of aging by doing the work itself. Without the Joy, the Hotpoint range, or the General Electric refrigerator, women were told, they faced the fate of their grandmothers on the farm: a rapid decline into premature old age.

In general, from the turn of the century through the 1920s, the dominant tendency in national advertising was to contrast the smooth highway of corporate-sponsored progress with the rut of rural tradition. Advertising, according to this view, helped lift the folk from their age-old somnolence into the "wide-awake" world of the 20th century. Far from weakening character, J. George

Frederick argued in 1925, "*advertising tends, of psychic necessity, to strengthen character.*" In his view, there were fewer "simple simons and docile doras" than in times past because "an environment replete with all imaginable merchandise *has compelled a toughening and sophistication of mental and even moral fiber.*"[33] Bruce Barton, in characteristically biblical cadences, also praised national advertisers as the agents of progress.

> The General Electric Company and the Western Electric Company find the people in darkness and leave them in light; the American Radiator finds them cold and leaves them warm; International Harvester finds them bending over their sickles the way their grandfathers did and leaves them riding triumphantly over their fields. The automobile companies find a man shackled to his front porch with no horizon beyond his own door yard and they broaden his horizon and make him in travel the equal of a king.[34]

Advertising was the engine of uplift, in Barton's view, because, "it stimulates desire. It makes people conscious of wants, and until you have wants you have no progress." Juxtaposing the divine discontent induced by mass-production with the bovine complacency of preindustrial societies, Barton fell into the pattern of most national advertisers, presenting rural life before the coming of advertised commodities as a reign of isolation, stasis, and intellectual death.[35]

From the 1890s through the 1920s, the imagery of national advertising increasingly constituted a seamless web of smooth-surfaced affluence, a bizarre symbolic universe where elegant young men and women dressed for dinner and never let the servants see them sweat. ("You always look so cool," Daisy Buchanan tells Jay Gatsby in *The Great Gatsby*. "'You resemble the advertisement of the man,' she went on innocently, 'you know the advertisement of the man. . . .'"[36] It was a world as insulated from common life as the advertisers' own experience—an inflation of elite male fantasies into a national norm. And it was a far cry from the actual or imagined lives of the American folk.[37]

Woman is the great civilizer. If it were not for her man would revert to whiskers and carry a club.

Woman does much for the Gillette because it is her presence, her influence, that puts the emphasis on good clothes, clean linen, and a clean shave.

She admires the clean, healthy skin of the man who uses a Gillette. She does not approve the ladylike massage-finish of the tonsorial artist. The massaged appearance ceased to be "class" largely because she said so. There is something fine and wholesome about the Gillette shave. It does not reek of violet water and pomades.

The use of the Gillette has a decidedly good effect on the skin. It gives a healthy look that suggests the outdoor rather than the indoor man.

Then think of the comfort—the convenience—the morning shave in less time than the morning dip.

A million men will buy Gillettes this year. Now is the time to get yours.

Standard Set with twelve double-edge blades, $5.00. Regular box of 12 blades, $1.00; carton of 6 blades, 50c.

King C Gillette

GILLETTE SALES COMPANY, 80 W. Second Street, Boston
New York, Times Bldg.   Chicago, Stock Exchange Bldg.   Gillette Safety Razor, Ltd., London   Eastern Office, Shanghai, China   Canadian Office, 63 St. Alexander St., Montreal
Factories: Boston, Montreal, Leicester, Berlin, Paris

Gillette Safety Razor Company advertisement. From *Town and Country*, October 22, 1910. Courtesy of the Boston Public Library.

Within two years of the stock market crash of 1929, the symbolic universe of advertising had begun to change dramatically. Cigarettes and luxury cars continued to win endorsements from polo players and ingenues, but commercial imagery as a whole no longer displayed the same uniform sheen of upper-class sophistication. Madison Avenue quickly felt the effects of the crash: as failing corporate clients cut advertising appropriations, agencies sent copywriters packing and slashed the salaries of those who remained. Many newer agencies, born in the boom years, folded altogether in the intensifying struggle for increasingly scarce billings. It was about this time that advertisers *en masse* rediscovered the virtues of straight talk to plain people. "The day of the dilettante is gone," a McCann-Erickson account executive announced, little more than a year after the crash. "The hard-boiled boys who know the business from the bottom up are now in the front office."[38] The "hard-boiled boys" aimed to reconnect advertising with ordinary people, but that effort could lead toward either a screaming tabloid style or a softer evocation of folk virtue. The first tactic reflected the mounting frenzy of copywriters straining to keep their jobs and agencies competing for scarce client dollars; the second embodied more complex cultural tendencies.[39]

Advertisers' rediscovery of the folk in the 1930s was part of a broader recovery of reassuring imagery in the face of economic crisis. The turn toward the past, the celebration of rural or small-town virtue linked commercial iconography with WPA murals, Frank Capra films, even the music of Aaron Copland and the choreography of Martha Graham. All resurrected folk culture as a resource for national regeneration. Advertisers' motives may not have been so exalted, but they dimly sensed the truth that Franklin Roosevelt articulated in his first inaugural address: that the dominant reaction to the Depression was fear. As Warren Susman has argued, a great many mass-cultural forms in the 1930s can be understood as attempts to restore a sense of psychic security to people who had felt "the bottom drop out."[40]

Advertisers, despite powerful countertendencies, participated in that restoration project. As early as 1931, the trade press suggested that artists and copywriters might look toward the past to locate reassuring imagery. "Perhaps the Campaign Demands an 'Old-Fashioned' Atmosphere," a *Printers' Ink* contributor wondered in 1931, as he noted advertisers' growing need to embody their "soundness" in representations to the public.[41] By mid-decade, according to the conventional wisdom, cleverness was out and plain speech in; trade journals advised advertisers to address "Grandma Jones, Buyer," who was more concerned with "comfortable living" than with fashion. Corporate food processors shifted their emphasis from purity to "home-cooked flavor";

Hurff's Soup, for example, took consumers into the enveloping warmth of the rural hearthside rather than the sterility of the scientifically managed kitchen. A naive viewer of such an advertisement (if any such viewer existed) would never have known that the commodity in question was sold in cans and mass-produced. The evocation of rural life was part of a wider tendency to sanctify familiar domestic ideals, to resurrect the home as a refuge from the ravages of an unforgiving economic climate; several years into the Depression, women in advertisements were stockier and more maternal than they had been during the 1920s. At the same time, other advertisers joined food processors in linking mass-produced goods with preindustrial craftsmanship and kin solidarity.

By 1936, *Fortune* magazine was marveling at the tendency of national advertising to "bury its alert head in the sands of the past." Advertisers, like other symbol makers in the 1930s, had turned to a mythic version of the American past to validate their present identity. In part this look backward merely meant the recruiting of historical luminaries for testimonials; however, it also involved the more frequent and sympathetic evocation of an amorphous preindustrial folk.[42]

There is no question that this renascence of folk imagery was rooted in circumstances peculiar to the Depression: the collapse of confidence in capitalist-style modernization; the movements "back to the land" and "back to the home"; above all, the response of artists, intellectuals, and corporate image producers to popular longings for emotional security through collective identity—the construction of a native folk tradition, an "American Way of Life." The 1930s were far from a Red Decade; in many ways the period was less a time of popular radicalism than a profoundly conservative cultural moment, a time when the seeds were sown for the conformist nationalism of the 1940s and 1950s. Advertisers participated in the corporate appropriation of traditional values—religious belief, patriotism, family solidarity—to legitimate untraditional aims: a foreign policy geared toward global expansion and an economic policy of oligopolist development.

Hurff's Soup advertisement. From *Life* magazine, 1936. Photo: Jackson Lears. Courtesy of the University of Missouri Library.

Yet it would be unwise to trace advertisers' participation in the
folk revival exclusively to the cultural impact of the Depression.
Despite their rant of progress, the good burghers among the advertising fraternity had always harbored suspicions of fashionable
snobs and had often linked them with urban modernity. From the
1890s on, this countertendency had periodically surfaced in the
trade press, as contributors occasionally argued that most advertisements were too snobbish, that most Americans did not know
how to order expensive dinners or even how to play golf, and that
advertisers should knock off their high-hat ways before they pro-
voked a general consumer revolt. In 1908, for example, a *Printers'
Ink* editorial complained:

> Advertising copy is written snobbishly. Pictures in magazines show
> bankers taking a leisurely breakfast of Corn Flakes, with the clock
> pointing to 10 A.M. Arguments for athletic underwear give the im-
> pression that it is not suitable to anybody but the salaried man.
> Fashion plates show the American gentleman lounging at his club,
> or taking the steamer to Europe. No body talks directly to the men
> and women who work with their hands. An examination of current
> advertising would pretty nearly convince the investigator that ad-
> vertisers regard manual or mechanical labor as disgraceful.

Some advertisers feared, with ample justification, that "the workman" might dismiss advertising as mere propaganda for the "salaried man" and his ways.[43]

Given advertisers' dominant tendency to identify the path of
progress with their own upper-class habits, it was only a short step
(for skeptics) from suspicion of snobbery to suspicion of modernity. Advertisers from time to time acknowledged the pull of the
preindustrial past, recommending that certain products be promoted as "old-fashioned" or finely crafted or just like Mother used
to make. The country paper took a lot of abuse as the locus of the
"substitution evil" (the practice of substituting local for nationally
advertised brands), but the belief persisted that the really successful man could be reached only through that rural medium; according to trade press mythology, he only scanned the headlines

of the big-city papers but pored over the news from his boyhood home. Throughout the 1920s, advertisers' persistent (though often subterranean) sympathy for the folk flowed from this countercurrent of feeling for their own small-town pasts.[44]

Where this sentiment was most loudly voiced was not in the advertisements but in the "editorial matter" surrounding them—the fiction and feature stories in the national magazines: *Good Housekeeping*, *American* magazine, and the like. By the 1920s, the same magazines whose advertisements celebrated urban sophistication carried stories and editorials decrying it. Republican ideology returned, stripped of its political implications, as a tribute to small-town sincerity and wisdom. The dapper men who dominated the advertisements were the villains in didactic fiction—men such as Dabney Mason, from the *American* story of 1926, who "had the classic face and the poise from an Hellenic legend. But within he was a little man, concerned with forms and manners."[45] The Protestant/republican distrust of deceptive surfaces lingered even in the citadels of national advertising, the slick-paper magazines. The heroes and heroines of popular fiction were invariably simple folk—stolid, plainspoken, and content with their lot. Their fullest embodiment was Scattergood, hero of Clarence Budington Kelland's fictional series and fount of New England folk wisdom. Scattergood outwitted urban sharpies, dismissed feminists, and attributed the high divorce rate among the "summer people" to "silk stockin's and these here lipsticks." His presence seemed incongruous alongside the glittering wares in the ad columns.[46]

The gap between the modernizing impulse of the advertisements and the folkish ideology in the rest of the magazine became especially apparent when one man straddled the two worlds, as Bruce Barton did. Besides preparing snappy advertising copy, Barton served up heartwarming sentiment as an interviewer, editorial columnist, and—most notoriously—interpreter of Jesus as the first advertising man. He was capable of praising ads as engines of progress one week, lamenting the loss of rural contentment the next. A spokesman for the most "advanced" sector of the economy, the heavily capitalized and bureaucratically organized corporations, Barton nevertheless harbored sympathy for simple agrarian ways. At least he claimed to so often and in such stirring platitudes that one is forced to conclude he meant it.[47] Men like Barton and Kelland, nurturing their vision of an American folk, had a ready-made response to the Depression: it was a judgment on our puff-pastry ways, a warning to return to the simple life. The economic crisis did not create those sentiments; it returned them to the surface of popular discourse.

The resilience of folkish sentiment stemmed from various sources. One was a mild admixture of Anglo-Protestant nativism. As immigrant ranks swelled during the early 20th century, so did support for immigration restriction, which was finally mandated by Congress in 1924. The immigrants from southern and eastern Europe were in many ways truer representatives of the "folk society" popularized by Redfield, yet their entry was restricted by those who claimed to be defenders of a native-born American folk. As nativist agitation intensified, *American* contributors asked, "Shall We Let the Cuckoos Crowd Us Out of Our Nest?" and Barton (among others) fretted that "the descendants of Yankee traders" had yielded their enterprising spirit to "the sons of men who came over in steerage."[48] These anxieties were too diffuse to be dispelled by legislation. Images of a racially homogeneous folk culture persisted in popular fiction; Kelland believed that "we" loved Scattergood because "so many of us derive from that stock; because there is something in us which responds to the honest old New England strain. We like the old thoughts and the old decencies—and we grope for the safe and comfortable feeling of them in this age of traffic and haste and radio and jazz."[49] Ethnocentrism shaped an antimodern resentment and promoted a tendency to connect non-Anglo immigrants with an offensive urban culture. On the continent during these interwar years, the ethnocentric component in folkish sentiment carried sinister overtones as it became part of overtly anti-Semitic ideologies. In the United States, while advertising icons could resemble the Hilter *Jugend*, anti-Semitism was usually muted—a matter of private jokes and boardroom grumbling about the antics of "the Semitic tribes."[50]

Among the Anglo-Protestant managerial class, ethnocentric anxieties remained implicit but pervasive; they helped fuel the fascination with an imagined colonial past, an Anglo-folk utopia where blacks knew their place and immigrants were absent. Advertising executives participated with others of their class in this Anglophilia: they designed "colonial" (or fake Tudor) residences, searched for antiques in New England villages, supported the restoration of Colonial Williamsburg. The ethnocentrism in these ventures was perhaps more powerful for remaining implicit. At the J. Walter Thompson Company, Chairman Stanley Resor commissioned a colonial-style executive dining room in 1922; when the company moved to the Graybar Building (near Grand Central station) in 1927, the dining room was moved piece by piece and reassembled in the new quarters. Even at the height of the "prosperity decade," the people in the cockpits of modernity were eager to preserve some connection with their imagined preindustrial past. A desire to resurrect "the honest old New England strain," the republican ideal of social transparency, led to the recreation of sanitized historical artifacts.

Yet there was more to folkish sentiment than yearnings for Saxon purity. The most famous folk icons were black: Rastus, the Cream of Wheat man (b. 1893), and Aunt Jemima (b. 1890). It is easy to dismiss these figures as emblems of white disdain, but their meanings were multivalent. Without question, they epitomized a whole constellation of nurturant values associated with preindustrial household and community life. They provided sustenance; they took care of (white) people. In this they resembled Betty Crocker (b. 1921), the embodiment of old-fashioned neighborliness, or the Mennen Company's Aunt Belle (b. 1920): "Belle is a real person and that is her real name. She really understands

Cream of Wheat advertisement. From *Saturday Evening Post*, September 6, 1913. Courtesy of the Boston Public Library.

babies. She would like to correspond with you about your baby."[51] These figures were created by and for an uprooted suburban bourgeoisie; they may well have helped focus one of the deepest psychic needs of both advertisers and their audience: a longing to overcome the sense of separation and loss endemic in a mobile market society, to recreate in fantasy what could not be achieved in everyday life—a renewed connection with the *gemeinschaftliche* worlds of extended family, local neighborhood, and organic community. Their motives were too numerous to name, but perhaps the basic impulse was an effort to grope for moral and emotional bearings amid the flux of modernity by fabricating a stable point of origin— though the only materials available might be snippets from memory, half-formed wishes, and clichés from *Life* magazine.

Still, it would be ludicrous to treat any folk motifs in advertising as spontaneous outpourings of emotion. Each advertisement was part of a carefully orchestrated campaign, and there was a great deal of ironic distance between advertisers and the images they fashioned. As blacks or females (or both), the folk icons fit the familiar role projected for the Other in the white male imagination: like the ideal Victorian woman, they could remain static, sheltering timeless values so that "progressive" men could ignore them in the forward rush to the future.

The distance between advertisers and advertisements becomes even more apparent when we consider that through the 1930s, most copywriters continued to hold their audience in contempt. As William Esty of J. Walter Thompson asserted in 1930, Captain John Smith's description of Indians in 17th-century Virginia still fit the vast majority of people in 20th-century America. Both populations were composed of "poor and miserable souls, wrapped up unto death in almost invincible ignorance." Let us not mince words, said Esty to his colleagues. "We say the Hollywood people are stupid, the pictures are stupid: what we are really saying is that the great bulk of people are stupid."[52] Concepts of mass behavior were fashionable with good reason in the 1930s; they helped explain the rise of fascism. But they also underwrote a broader dismissal of popular intelligence. Some of the same people who were publicly celebrating the common man were privately dis-

Aunt Jemima Pancake Flour advertisement. From *Saturday Evening Post,* August 28, 1920. Courtesy of the Boston Public Library.

missing him as an intellectual cipher. Psychological theory reinforced that attitude. The father of behaviorist theory, John B. Watson, went to work for J. Walter Thompson in 1920, and continued to hammer home the point that "we have nothing to work with except a public vast and inert and regulated by emotion plus a very embryonic and weak reasoning faculty."[53] Despite occasional efforts to defend the good sense of the consumer, the mass of advertising opinion supported the conclusion that advertisers were superior to their audience.

The gulf between copywriter and consumer existed in copywriters' own minds if not in actuality; it suggests that folk motifs in national advertising might profitably be viewed not only as projections of elite male fantasies but also as another instance of a recurring rhetorical strategy. No matter how fervently they chanted the gospel of newness, advertisers knew they had to establish some common ground, some sense of old-shoe familiarity between the purchaser and the product. Folk motifs served that purpose. They allowed the adepts of progress to have it both ways—to assert that the best of traditional values survived even as modernization whirled ahead at full tilt. An Eveready Radio battery advertisement of 1929, headed "Sunday Evening," typified the genre. Once, the copy began, the only entertainment allowed on Sunday evening was tedious organ playing by Sis. It was a time of "desperate boredom":

> No one was allowed to laugh and play. . . . Such were Sunday evenings years ago. But, today, Sunday evening is looked forward to with pleasure. The children anticipate its coming. The thundering music of a great church organ thrills them . . . a famous minister warms the whole family by his message of hope and cheer . . . all join in with the grand old hymns that come over the air . . . *for now they have a radio set*! . . . The rest of the week is just as full of interest! . . . *You can never be isolated from the world with a radio in your home*!

What comes over the radio on Sunday evening is not the fundamentalist folk religion, but the optimistic liberal Protestantism of the suburban upper classes. "The children," being a step closer to the pace set by advertising, find this newer creed especially appealing; but the "whole family" is "warmed" by it—perhaps especially because "the grand old hymns" are still in place. From this peculiarly eclectic (perhaps "postmodern") view, anything of value in the past ("the grand old hymns") was preserved and even enhanced among the new world of goods, while the vast bulk of past experience—poverty, isolation, and "desperate boredom"—could be jettisoned with relief. No worthwhile tradition was lost en route to modernity.[54]

That was the key move in advertising's rhetorical appropriation of folk values: the innovator presented himself as a traditionalist at heart; the mortal enemy of folklife declared he or she was its chief defender. This had been a successful gambit of modernizers for over a century. The federalist orator Tench Coxe had used it in 1787, when he argued that the adoption of the factory system would enhance rather than erode republican values by insulating Americans from the corrupting influence of European manufactured goods. *Atlanta Constitution* editor Henry Grady employed a similar approach in the 1880s: urging industrialization, he supported his New South creed with the assertion that the factory system was not the betrayal but the fulfillment of the Old South's chivalric ideals. But the people who brought this strategy to full fruition were the rhetoricians employed by the modern corporation. In selling home-cooked canned goods, promoting mass-produced craftsmanship, or linking fast-food meals with "family values," 20th-century advertisers have turned the trick on a scale that Coxe and Grady could hardly have imagined.[55]

However the audience responded to this pseudo-traditionalist pose, the largest cultural implications of the strategy were corrosive. By incorporating the folk, advertising falsely assimilated past or passing ways of life with modernity. Like the straightforward celebration of modernity, the incorporation of the folk devalued the rural past by denying it any separate ontological status. When

The Craftsman's Mastership

SOME men are slaves to work; others are masters of it. The first work to live; the second live to work.

Of the second type are artists and craftsmen. Their work is the supreme expression of their life, their spirit, their ideals. Only through it can they create. In it they find their keenest pleasures. Of its results they are its severest judges.

Due to the rugged character and natural creative genius of its people, New England has for nearly three hundred years offered the most fertile soil in America for the development of craftsmanship.

Generation after generation, New England artisans have been imbued with a spirit of mastership— independent, individualistic, proud, unshaken by industrial and social upheavals.

For nearly thirty years this spirit has governed the building of Stevens-Duryea Motor Cars.

Starting with the courage of pioneers, New England craftsmen and inventors produced a gasoline automobile that ran successfully under its own power in 1892. They have contributed to the industry many of its most important fundamental principles. They are building a car today which throughout its beautiful whole is worthy to be known as their masterwork.

STEVENS-DURYEA, Inc.
Chicopee Falls, Massachusetts

Stevens-Duryea
Motor Cars
30th Year

Stevens-Duryea automobiles advertisement. From *Saturday Evening Post*, August 28, 1920. Courtesy of the Boston Public Library.

modernization was exalted, the folk were merely a foil for the exciting present and future; when the folk were invoked, the advertisers implicitly denied any rupture between tradition and modernity, trivialized the challenge of the past to the present, and ignored the destructive effects of change. Their outlook resembled the evolutionary progressiveness of Teilhard de Chardin, whose slogan they would have loved, if they had ever read it: "Nothing is ever lost to the race."[56]

The denial of loss is not "nostalgia" but the erasure of its basis—and what may, indeed, be the basis of all historical memory under modern cultural conditions: the sense of the pastness of the past, the radical disjunction between "then" and "now." Advertisers' contempt for the past and fabrication of spurious substitutes for it led Frankfurt School theorists such as Theodor Adorno and Herbert Marcuse to charge that commercial mass culture (and advertising most perniciously) had promoted a kind of cultural amnesia. The charge is worth pondering; certainly few economic systems are more dedicated than American-style capitalism to the obliteration of the past as the material embodiment of everyday life. The instrumentalist mentality behind this rejection of the past is perhaps summed up in a comment from a J. Walter Thompson staff member at a meeting in the early 1930s: "The only reason that any normal minded man or woman is interested in a year that is past is probably because of what they [sic] learned in the year that will be of service in the future."[57] This was hardly an attitude calculated to enhance memory in any but the most narrowly pragmatic sense. Advertisers' progressive ideology involved, at least for some, the systematic cultivation of forgetfulness. This forgetfulness could enhance what Milan Kundera and other novelists have identified as a peculiar feature of modern sensibility—an "unbearable lightness of being" that both excites and depresses the modernizer on his or her headlong flight from past to future.[58]

Yet, even though the incorporation of the folk smoothed the assimilation of progressive assumptions, it also kept antimodern discontent alive. The use of folk motifs could succeed as a rhetorical strategy only if some traditionalist assumptions (however vague) lingered in the minds of the audience. Something really has been lost in transit to industrial modernity, the ads seem to suggest, some direct, sincere or "folk" quality, and *we* have miraculously preserved it—authenticity amid artifice, all the charms of yesterday amid the comforts of tomorrow. Whatever the audience thought of the redemptive powers of the particular product, the implication of a wider loss was unmistakable. In a culture dedicated to denying the costs of development, that sense of loss could have subversive consequences. At the least it could lead to a silent dissent from current cant. The notion of a traditional past, the vision of a folk society—though they may not conform any longer to the canons of empirical scholarship, those ideas still play a salutary role in promoting a skeptical attitude toward the corporate agenda of progress. For who among us hasn't ventured the belief—or hope—that, once, it was *different*, back then?

NOTES

1. See Ferdinand Tönnies, *Gemeinschaft und Gesellschaft (Community and Society)* [1887], trans. and ed. Charles P. Loomis (East Lansing: Michigan State University Press, 1957); Max Weber, *The Protestant Ethic and the Spirit of Capitalism* [1904] trans. Talcott Parsons (New York: Scribner's, 1958). The *Communist Manifesto* is of course available in numerous reprints. I used Karl Marx and Friedrich Engels, "Manifesto of the Communist Party" [1848] in Lewis Feuer, edition, *Marx and Engels: Basic Writing on Politics and Philosophy*, (New York: Doubleday, 1954), p. 11.
2. The most sophisticated critique of the quest for community in American scholarship is Thomas Bender, *Community and Social Change in America* (Baltimore and London: Johns Hopkins University Press, 1982). See also the probing comments by Raymond Williams, *The Country and the City* (New York: Oxford University Press, 1973), esp. pp. 1–13. The most striking example of community as methodological fiction is Robert Wiebe, *The Search for Order, 1877–1920* (New York: Hill & Wang, 1967). The quotation is from Carl Degler, *Out of Our Past*, rev. ed. (New York: Harper & Row, 1970), p. 1.
3. On the popular construction of the past, see the magisterial work by David Lowenthal, *The Past Is a Foreign Country* (Cambridge, England: Cambridge University Press, 1985).
4. See, for example, Robert Redfield, *The Folk Culture of Yucatan* (Chicago: University of Chicago Press, 1941), his more flexible formulation in *The Little Community* (Chicago: University of Chicago Press, 1955), and the classic essay by Louis Wirth, "Urbanism as a Way of Life," *American Journal of Sociology* 44 (1938), 1–24.
5. Rodney Olsen, "The Sentimental Idiom in Victorian Culture," (colloquium presented at National Museum of American History, Smithsonian Institution, Washington, D. C., March 17, 1987.)

6. Jean Starobinski, "The Idea of Nostalgia," *Diogenes* 54 (1966): 81–103.

7. The literature on republican ideology is enormous, but the two essential works remain Bernard Bailyn, *The Ideological Origins of the American Revolution* (Cambridge, Mass.: Harvard University Press, 1967), and Gordon Wood, *The Creation of the American Republic, 1776–1787* (Chapel Hill: University of North Carolina Press, 1969).

8. On the persistence of republican ideals, see, for example Bruce Laurie, *The Working People of Philadelphia, 1800–1850* (Philadelphia: Temple University Press, 1980); Steven Hahn, *The Roots of Southern Populism: Yeoman Farmers and the Transformation of the Georgia Upcountry, 1850–1890* (New York: Oxford University Press, 1983); and Sean Wilentz, *Chants Democratic: New York City and the Rise of the American Working Class, 1788–1850* (New York: Oxford University Press, 1984).

9. For surveys of this incipient media culture, see Peter Marzio, *The Democractic Art: Chromolithography, 1840–1900* (Boston: Godine, 1979), and Robert Jay, *The Trade Card in Nineteenth Century America* (Columbia: University of Missouri Press, 1987).

10. For examples, see parlor organ trade cards in Book 16C, Bella C. Landauer Collection, New-York Historical Society; Allen's Root Beer Extract (1882) in Beverages, Box 1, Warshaw Collection of Business Americana, National Museum of American History, Smithsonian Institution; Akron Milling Company (c. 1890) in Cereals, Box 41, Warshaw Collection; Walter Wood Implements (1894) in Agriculture, Box 6, Warshaw Collection; Union Club Coffee (1892) in Coffee, Box 1, Warshaw Collection; Anger Baking Company (c. 1885) in Bakers and Baking, Box 1, Warshaw Collection; B. Wild & Company (c. 1895) in Confectionery, Box 96, Warshaw Collection; American Cereal Company, *America's Cereal Foods and How To Cook Them* (Ravenna, Ohio: 1893), front cover, in Cereals, Box 41, Warshaw Collection.

11. Wooldridge Fertilizer, *Farmer and Planters Almanac* (Hagerstown, Md.: 1891), cover, Fertilizer, Box 8, Warshaw Collection; McCormick Reaper Company Catalogue (1894), cover, Agriculture, Box 4, Warshaw Collection.

12. Vick's Floral Guide (1885), Agriculture, Box 14, Warshaw Collection; William Deering & Company, trade cards (1891), Agriculture, Box 8, Warshaw Collection; Skandia Plow Company, trade cards (c. 1880), Agriculture, Box 12, Warshaw Collection.

13. Dr. Greene, *Nervous Diseases* (privately printed, 1887), in Patent Medicines, Landauer Collection.

14. G. G. Green, Makers of Boschee's German Syrup, *Census and Diary Almanac* (Woodbury, N. J.: 1881–1914), in Patent Medicines, Box 11, Warshaw Collection; Pond's Extract, trade cards (1879), in Patent Medicines, Box 26, Warshaw Collection; J. C. Childs Company, trade cards (c. 1890) in Patent Medicines, Box 6, Warshaw Collection; Dr. Petzold's German Bitters, trade cards (1884), in Patent Medicines, Box 25, Warshaw Collection. On the consolidation of medical authority, see Paul Starr, *The Social Transformation of American Medicine* (New York: Basic Books, 1982) esp. chaps. 1–3.

15. N. C. Thompson Company, trade cards (c. 1895), in Agriculture, Box 13, Warshaw Collection; Duke's Cigarettes, trade card, in Tobacco Products, Box A-G, Warshaw Collection.

16. On the antimarket impluse behind Prohibition, see Norman Clark, *Deliver Us From Evil: An Interpretation of American Prohibition* (New York: Norton, 1976) and Jack Blocker, *Retreat from Reform: The Prohibition Movement in the United States* (Westport, Conn.: Greenwood, 1976).

17. "Advertising Agents and the Country Press," *Printers' Ink* 13 (August 21, 1895): 44–45; "Ready-Made Advertisements," *Printers' Ink* 48 (August 10, 1904): 60–61; "Passing of the Country Weekly," *Printers' Ink* 36 (July 31, 1901): 14; John S. Grey, "Dr. Pierce's Advertising," *Printers' Ink* 25 (November 16, 1898): 34–35; Marco Morrow, "The Country Paper," *Printers' Ink* 22 (February 9, 1898): 8; "Some Recollections of a Country Publisher," *Printers' Ink* 51 (June 7, 1905): 27–28; "The Country Editor's Side," *Printers' Ink* 19 (May 26, 1897): 8. For more general treatments of

urban-rural conflict during this period, see Fred A. Shannon, *The Farmer's Last Frontier, 1860–1897* (New York: Farrar & Rinehart, 1945); Earl W. Hayter, *The Troubled Farmer* (Dekalb: Northern Illinois University Press, 1968); and David Danbom, *The Resisted Revolution: Urban America and the Industrialization of Agriculture, 1900–1930* (Ames: Iowa State University Press, 1979).

18. On the social background of agency personnel, see Rowland Marchand, *Advertising the American Dream: Making Way for Modernity, 1920–1940* (Berkeley: University of California Press, 1984), pp. 130–138. On the rise of advertising professionalism, see Jackson Lears, "Some Versions of Fantasy: Toward a Cultural History of American Advertising, 1880–1930" in Jack Salzman, editor, *Prospects: an Annual of American Culture Studies* (New York: Cambridge University Press, 1984), pp. 363–368.

19. Wolstan Dixey, "Dramatic Effect in Advertising" *Printers' Ink* 21 (November 24, 1897): 16; "'Spotless Town,'" *Printers' Ink* 35 (April 10, 1901): 24; John Starr Hewitt, "The Copywriter's Workbench," in J. George Frederick, ed., *Masters of Advertising Copy* (New York: Business Bourse, 1925), p. 323.

20. *The J. Walter Thompson Book* (New York: 1909), pp. 8–9, (J. Walter Thompson Company Archives), New York.

21. J. Walter Thompson, *The Red Ear* (New York: privately printed, c. 1880), n.p.

22. Alphonsus P. Haire, "The Farmer and His 'Benzine Buggy,'" *Printers' Ink* 62 (March 25, 1908): 10–15; "How Adler Proved that Farmers Want Snappy Clothes," *Printers' Ink* 72 (July 14, 1914): 52–54. See also "Reaching the Rural Classes," *Judicious Advertising* 1 (March 1903): 27–29.

23. Wooldridge Fertilizer Co., *Farmers and Planters Almanac* (Hagerstown, Md., 1891), 74, in Fertilizer, Box 8, Warshaw Collection.

24. See, for example, *Spirit of the Times* (New York) 1, no. 20 (April 28, 1832): 4.

25. National Biscuit Company, advertisement, *Saturday Evening Post* 177 (November 5, 1904), back cover.

26. Scull's Coffee, advertisements (1900), Book 133 in N. W. Ayer Collection, National Museum of American History, Smithsonian Institution; Lion Coffee, advertisements (1905), in Book 132, Ayer Collection.

27. Genessee Pure Food Company, pamphlets for Jell-O (c. 1905) in Foods, Box 13, Warshaw Collection; Knox Dainty Desserts for Dainty People, advertisements (1915), in Foods, Box 13, Warshaw Collection; Holsom Bread, advertisements (c. 1915) in Book 256, Ayer Collection, Dromedary Dixie-Mix, advertisement, *Good Housekeeping* 99 (December 1934): 203.

28. Meadow Gold Butter, advertisement (1909), in Book 128, Ayer Collection.

29. Central City Soap Company, advertisements (1904–1906) in Book 232, Ayer Collection.

30. Ruth Schwartz Cowan, *More Work for Mother: The Ironies of Household Technology from the Open Hearth to the Microwave* (New York: Basic Books, 1983).

31. On this point, see Glenna Matthews, *"Just a Housewife": The Rise and Fall of Domesticity in the United States* (New York: Oxford University Press, 1987).

32. Louisville Food Products, advertisements for Clean-Easy and Joy (1919–1920), in Book 233, Ayer Collection. See also Miller's Soap advertisements (1903–1905) in Book 232, Ayer Collection and Maple City Soap Works, advertisements (1905–1906) in Book 232, Ayer Collection.

33. J. George Frederick, "The Story of Ad Writing," in *Masters of Advertising Copy*, pp. 35–37, emphasis in original.

34. Barton, "Human Appeals in Copy," in ibid., 66–67.

35. Barton, "The New Business World," transcript of radio address in Barton Papers, Wisconsin State Historical Society, Madison.

36. F. Scott Fitzgerald, *The Great Gatsby* (New York: Scribners & Sons, 1953), p. 119.

37. On the class-bound quality of advertising's symbolic universe, see Lears, "Some Versions," pp. 380–382, and Marchand, *Advertising the American Dream*, chapter 6.

38. John J. McCarthy, "Shirt Sleeve Executives," *Printers' Ink* 154 (March 12, 1931): 58–67.

39. For the impact of the Depression, see Marchand, *Advertising the American Dream*, pp. 286–287.

40. Warren Susman, *Culture as History* (New York: Pantheon, 1984), pp. 150–210. For an incisive account of the impulse to capture "ordinary" lives, see William Stott, *Documentary Expression and Thirties America* (New York: Oxford University Press, 1973).

41. Kenneth Grosbeck, "When Advertising Returns to the Simple Life," *Printers' Ink* 158 (January 14, 1932): 3–6, 112–113.

42. G. B. Larrabee, "Grandma Jones, Buyer," ibid. 167 (May 3, 1934): 29–36; John J. McCarthy, "Back to Homespun," ibid. 158 (March 31, 1932): 17–21; "There's No Place Like Home," ibid. 159 (May 12, 1932): 65; Roy Dickinson, "Getting Down to Fundamentals," ibid. 162 (January 12, 1933): 25–26; "Advertising Looks Backward," *Fortune* (January 13, 1936): 6.

43. "Arguments for the Workman," *Printers' Ink* 64 (August 12, 1908): 19.

44. Walter K. Mulhall, "Advertising a Product as Old-Fashioned," *Printers' Ink* 119 (May 4, 1922): 33–36; John Chester, "Country Newspapers," *Printers' Ink* 14 (January 29, 1896): 25; Joel Benton, "The Country Paper," *Printers' Ink* 18 (January 13, 1897): 24; "The Country Paper," *Printers' Ink* 17 (December 2, 1896): 3.

45. Melville D. Post, "The Invisible Client," *American* 102 (December 1926): 23.

46. Clarence Budington Kelland, "Paper Flowers," *American* 113 (May 1932): 69.

47. I have discussed Barton at length in "From Salvation to Self-realization: Advertising and the Therapeutic Roots of the Consumer Culture, 1880–1930," in Richard Fox and Jackson Lears, editors, *The Culture of Consumption: Critical Essays in American History, 1880–1980* (New York: Pantheon, 1983), pp. 3–38.

48. Owen Wister, "Shall We Let the Cuckoos Crowd Us Out of Our Nest?" *American* 91 (March, 1921): 47; Bruce Barton, "Courage to Dive Off the Dock," *American* 94 (August 1922): 24.

49. C. B. Kelland, "The Inside Story of Scattergood," *American* (October 1926): 74.

50. J. Walter Thompson Company Creative Staff Meeting, Minutes, December 7, 1932, in JWT Archives.

51. Mennen Company, advertisement, *Good Housekeeping* 71 (July-August 1920): 114. On these trademarks and their history, see Hal Morgan, *Symbols of America* (New York: Viking, 1986), pp. 7, 55, 126.

52. William Esty at J. Walter Thompson Company group meeting, September 30, 1930, in JWT Archives.

53. John B. Watson, address to Standard Brands sales training class, April 27, 1931, in JWT Archives.

54. Eveready Radio Batteries, advertisement (1929), in Box 37, Ayer Collection. Emphasis in original.

55. On Tench Coxe, see John Kasson, *Civilizing the Machine: Technology and Republican Values in America, 1776–1900* (New York and London: Penguin, 1977) pp. 28–32. Paul Gaston discusses Henry Grady in *The New South Creed* (New York: Knopf, 1970).

56. Quoted in Brother Antoninus, "Our Modern Sensibility," *Commonweal* 77 (October 26, 1962): 12.

57. Hugh Baillie at J. Walter Thompson Company representatives' meeting, January 6, 1931, in JWT Archives.

58. Milan Kundera, *The Unbearable Lightness of Being*, transl. Michael Heim (New York: Harper & Row, 1984).

Modernism, Edith Halpert, Holger Cahill, and the Fine Art Meaning of American Folk Art

EUGENE W. METCALF, JR.
❦ and ❧
CLAUDINE WEATHERFORD

I N HIS ARTICLE, "The Impact of the Concept of Culture on the Concept of Man," anthropologist Clifford Geertz remarks that human nature is necessarily specific. Instead of being universal and constant, the essence of humans is so entangled with their particular times, places, and circumstances that it is inseparable from them. Humans must rely to a large extent on cultural mechanisms to govern thought and behavior. Such mechanisms are specific to the societies in which they operate, and are the historically created systems of meaning that humans use to give form, order, and direction to their lives.[1]

In any society, at a given time, certain meanings assume special importance because they articulate significant issues which need to be addressed and conventionalized. Such meanings are central to the development and maintenance of key patterns of culture. These meanings express what is unique about a particular society: accordingly, understanding the nature of these meanings helps unlock the significance of social behavior.

In American society, since at least the opening decades of this century, one significant meaning has been the concept of the folk. By developing and popularizing this meaning, and by manipulating the symbols that express it, Americans have been involved in structuring and coming to grips with their experience in the con-

141

temporary world. The concept of folk has been synthesized in a broad range of cultural activities, artifacts, and ideas, and as such has become an important factor in defining the nature and significance of modern America. Yet of all the cultural arenas that have incorporated the concept of folk, none has been more important than the arts. For it has been as an aesthetic vision that the meaning of the folk has achieved one of its most popular and powerful contemporary American forms.

Art represents and sanctifies what is valued in modern society; it imparts both cultural authority and importance to particular ideas and images. This authority attaches not only to the objects designated as art, but also to those who create and appreciate such objects, giving them social status and honor. John Berger has argued that art's authority derives in part from the fact that art is thought to exist within a special preserve. Originally this preserve may have been magical or sacred, but in modern society it became social as art fell into the custody of the leisured, elite classes where it became representative of their social status.[2] Such art came to be honored as "fine art," and distinguished from other less status-laden objects of human manufacture, being defined largely in terms of its aesthetic qualities, qualities that emphasize its association with contemplation and leisure rather than with production and work.

Yet fine art performs many other social functions in addition to bestowing status, and it is in terms of one of these functions that the meaning of folk comes to have particular cultural importance. Dissociated from the world of necessary labor, fine art is celebrated for its ability to transcend the experience of everyday life. Such art is said to exist above mere social concerns and to speak to universal issues. Thus set apart from mundane reality, the realm of art becomes a cultural arena in which normally rigid systems of social meaning are relaxed.

As Constance Perin has suggested, the human ability to tolerate ambiguity is remarkably limited. Clinging tenaciously to the familiar and shared systems of meaning that give order and structure to our lives, we normally resist and reject experiences of novelty and uncertainty that threaten our ability to render the world meaningful. Indeed, says Perin, in modern society it is perhaps only in the realm of the fine arts that we have become accustomed to welcoming ambiguity, and then it takes continual practice as well as constant prodding and assistance from teachers, critics, and catalogues.[3] People who are the most receptive to the intrusion of artistic ambiguity are generally those who accept, or aspire to, the elite standards and values that support fine art. Although these people value art for its transformative power, its ability to "reorganize experience" and to "change the way we look at things," such changes are generally accepted only if they can be understood in terms of pre-existing aesthetic values. Moreover, since these changes are confined to the special preserve of art—a place disconnected from the realm of everyday life—they cannot immediately threaten established systems of social meaning.

Yet as much as humans resist or fear the disorientation that results from the alteration of accepted patterns of social meaning, such experience is inevitable and necessary. Patterns of culture change and evolve and, as philosopher Morse Peckham has suggested, in modern society the experience of fine art may offer for middle- and upper-class groups an important way to deal with such necessary but threatening changes. According to Peckham:

> Art is rehearsal for those real situations in which it is vital for our survival to endure cognitive tension. . . . Art is the reinforcement of the capacity to endure disorientation so that a real and significant problem may emerge. Art is the exposure to the tensions and problems of a false world so that man may endure exposing himself to the tensions and problems of the real world.[4]

Seen in this perspective, the incorporation of the idea of the folk into the concept of fine art that took place in American society in the first decades of the 20th century was a significant cultural event. Identified in terms of many unsettling social issues that were confronting and confounding America at this time, the meaning of the folk—as it came to be comprehended in fine art terms—helped rationalize the cultural and social tension these issues were provoking. Encompassing and synthesizing the often contradictory meanings of the past and present, the view of folk art, as it was developed and popularized, helped establish new conventions for understanding and coping with modern experience, and was thus involved with giving form to the modern American self.[5]

Folk art was discovered in America in the second and third decades of this century during a time of rapid and disquieting social change. One of the most important of these changes was the growth of the city as America completed the transition from a rural to an urban nation. In the minds of many Americans rural life now appeared dull and sterile. Yet as much as Americans seemed to welcome the glamour and vitality of the city, they also feared encroaching urbanization. To a nation raised on Jeffersonian ideals, the city still represented images of sin and decay. It was a place of debauchery and crowding, a haven for crime and unassimilated foreigners. Such conflicting hopes and fears were not new to America, but in these years they were deeply felt, and they represented an ambivalence that affected other social issues.

Although Americans welcomed the consumer goods made available through new industrial techniques, such as the moving assembly line and the widespread use of the electrical motor, they were also uneasy with the technology that produced these goods. Fear of dehumanization and standardization was part of the general reaction to the machines' effect on modern life, and Americans often voiced the fear that man himself was becoming little more than a machine—a robot to use a word that developed at that time.

Demographic and technological changes exacerbated other alterations in American life, such as those that occurred in religious practices, family structure, and patterns of immigration, creating a culture that felt deeply threatened despite its prosperity. Battered by the forces of change, and unable to make sense of contemporary events through the use of old systems of belief and feeling, Americans struggled to develop new conventions to accommodate modern experience, and new symbols to mark and contain emerging categories of meaning. In a world that was now suddenly inundated with, and dazzled by, consumer goods, it is not surprising that one of the powerful symbolic devices that began to develop in the teens and 1920s for explaining and integrating American experience would itself eventually become popularized in the 1930s as a new commodity—American folk art.

Folk art first came to the attention of a consuming public in the teens when Hamilton Easter Field, a wealthy artist, critic, and collector, introduced the objects that would become known as folk art in fine art circles. An ardent proponent of the self-expression and vigorous individualism that would be a hallmark of modern artists, Field was one of the prominent supporters and patrons of artists who were inclined to deviate from the practices of the conservative National Academy. While traveling and studying art in Europe in the first decades of the century, Field had become acquainted with Asian and African art, as well as with the work of modernists like Picasso. Fascinated with these objects, Field began to collect them, and in 1909 commissioned a mural from Picasso for the library of his home in Brooklyn.[6] To support and promote his vision of modern art, in 1913 Field established the Ogunquit School of Painting and Sculpture on the southern coast of Maine and later, in 1916, extended his teaching program by opening the Ardsley School of Modern Art in Brooklyn. Field also operated an exhibition space in Brooklyn called Ardsley Studios, which showed and promoted the works of such modern artists as John Marin, Marsden Hartley, Marguerite and William Zorach, Robert Laurent, Man Ray, Charles Demuth, Max Weber, Bernard Karfiol, and Abraham Walkowitz. In 1918, Field became a member and officer of the Society of Independent Artists and opened his studio to that group. During this period he also advocated the cause of modern art through his work as an art critic and writer in such magazines and newspapers as the *Brooklyn Daily Eagle, Art and Decoration*, and *The Arts*, which he founded in 1920.

Field's eclectic aesthetic tastes included not only modern, Asian, and African art, but also the art of children. Like Alfred Stieglitz, who had first exhibited children's art at his gallery "291" in 1912, Field was attracted to such art because of its lack of artifice, its instinctiveness, and its natural qualities. He also found these qualities, as well as many of the formal values of modern art, in the paintings of 18th-century itinerant artists. In 1921, for example, Field wrote that a portrait titled *Catalina Schuyler* "might almost be a late Picasso," and he even applied some of the same aesthetic criteria to the early American chairs and tables he collected. Such decorative arts, Field said, are "the expression of the soul of the people," and his aesthetic appreciation of them could be seen not only in his home, where he displayed individual pieces of furniture as art objects, but also in his magazine *The Arts*, for which he wrote articles on topics such as hooked rugs.[7]

When, with the help of friend and sculptor Robert Laurent, Field established the Ogunquit school in 1913, it was only natural that he would there express his aesthetic preferences. Field decorated the studios he rented to artists at Ogunquit with objects such as untutored paintings, carved decoys, and hooked rugs that he had obtained from local barns and antique shops. Like Field, many of his artist-tenants recognized in these objects the same qualities of vigor, simplicity, and abstraction that they were trying to produce in their own art. As a result, they also began to search for, and collect, similar things. Among these new collectors, none were more enthusiastic than Robert Laurent, William Zorach, Yasuo Kuniyoshi, and Bernard Karfiol. According to art dealer Edith Gregor Halpert, who first saw this folk art at Ogunquit in 1926 (four years after Field's death, when Laurent was operating the Ogunquit school), "Field was undeniably the pioneer in the field [for he was] responsible for directing attention to American folk art as an . . . aesthetic expression."[8]

For modern sculptors, who were battling the dominance of the French Ecole des Beaux Arts and its enshrinement in American sculpture as a primarily public and architectural form, Field's folk art collection was a revelation. Not only did it support these sculptors' desire for a fundamentally different sculptural vision, but it also embodied some of the principal challenges to the dominant sculptural ideal. As art historian Daniel Robbins has pointed out, the first of these challenges was the desire to de-monumentalize sculpture by increasing its production and purchase as a household item. Although this aim was not unique to the modernists (the National Sculpture Society had made it an organizational goal in its constitution of 1893),[9] it was still, in an era that enshrined sculpture as a public form, an unrealized hope. Thus, instead of working their way up in the world of sculpture through the then-accepted method of apprenticing themselves to established sculptors who could secure large architectural commissions for civic statuary, modernist sculptors such as Robert Laurent and William Zorach often chose to work by themselves to create less monumental and more personal forms, such as the animal sculpture that became especially popular in the 1920s.[10] Such works, like the folk carvings collected by these artists, could be easily collected and displayed in private homes; just as important, in this sculpture one could recognize the stamp of a personal vision.

A second and notable challenge to the Beaux Arts style was the developing interest in direct carving in stone, marble, or wood instead of modeling from clay. Often referred to as the "aesthetic of materials," direct carving was introduced into professional American sculpture through the efforts of Robert Laurent before the 1913 Armory Show, and further established in the early '20s with the work of William Zorach. Through their art and teaching (at the Ardsley School, Ogunquit, and the Art Students League), Laurent and Zorach inspired a whole generation of direct carvers:

by the 1930s the idea of direct carving had become a dominant one in modern sculpture. Often considered to be a legacy of John Ruskin, William Morris, and the Arts and Crafts Movement, which aimed to revive handcraftsmanship in an era of mechanization, this sculptural technique was also influenced by the example and efforts of the folk carvers so avidly collected by Laurent, Zorach, and their artist friends.[11]

Folk art was connected to modernist sculpture in a third way. According to Daniel Robbins, while artists working in the Beaux Arts tradition often regarded themselves as intellectuals and thinkers concerned primarily with the conceptualizing and modeling of spiritual values (whose translation into stone or marble could then be turned over to mere technicians), modernist sculptors involved in direct carving considered themselves workers whose art emerged through their dialogue with their material. As a result, not only did the modernists become interested in the techniques and products of so-called primitive art, but they came to believe that "great art could be immediately recognized by the untutored, that is, the mass of the people,"[12] a tenet that Hamilton Easter Field had applied to folk art.

The final, and perhaps most significant, challenge that folk art presented to Beaux Arts hegemony was an idea strenuously resisted by the American art establishment: that "form and space alone carry content, idea, and emotion without regard to representation."[13] Already well developed in Europe before the Armory Show, this concept was too threatening to the American tradition of public statuary to be taken seriously by most American sculptors until decades later. Nevertheless, introduced to America by immigrant artists such as Elie Nadelman and Alexander Archipenko, and expatriates such as Max Weber, this revolutionary idea eventually carried the day. In a way, through Nadelman's efforts, its victory was connected to the modernists' discovery of folk art.

Born in Poland in 1882, Nadelman studied art briefly in Warsaw and Cracow, then went to Munich and Paris. While in Germany and France, Nadelman became aware not only of trends in contemporary art, but also the antiquities of the Aegean and Mediterranean and the folk arts of Europe. With these as background, beginning in 1905 Nadelman focused his work on an issue that would consume his attention for the next 20 years: the reduction of human and animal forms to an irreducible profile.[14] He developed an abstract, curvilinear aesthetic system, one discordant with rectilinear cubism; yet Nadelman soon became a formidable presence in the Paris art world, where he knew Picasso and was acknowledged as one of the first to experiment with abstract form. Nadelman emigrated to America in 1914, where, according to art historian Roberta Tarbell, his presence

> was seminal, not only for the impact of the qualities of his sculpture, especially his abstracted curvilinear systems, but also for the importance of his theories of plasticity, beauty, and significant form. His reduction of figures to geometric, curved volumes and spaces, and the refinement of his ideas . . . appealed to and were echoed in the works of Lachaise, Robus, Zorach, Laurent and many other important American sculptors.[15]

Part of Nadelman's influence lay in the fact that in his work and ideas could be recognized many of the important aesthetic concerns that also drew the modernists to American folk art. Shortly after he arrived in the United States, Nadelman began collecting American folk art with a passion, and by 1924 he had amassed such a collection that he and his wife opened their own museum. During this period he came to understand American folk art in terms of issues that animated his own work—for example, aesthetic theories such as "significant form," an important modernist idea popularized by English art critic Clive Bell in 1914, but first presented by Nadelman in remarks published in *Camera Work* in 1910. Nadelman's remarks about his own work could have been equally applied to his understanding of folk art, an understanding that connected this art form with new aesthetic notions of modern abstraction. According to Nadelman, "The subject of any work is for me nothing but a pretense for creating significant forms, relations of forms which create a new life that has nothing to do with life in nature."[16]

Yet sculptors weren't the only modern artists who incorporated the idea of the folk into American fine art. Painters working at Ogunquit were also fascinated with American folk art. Bernard Karfiol and Yasuo Kuniyoshi reveled in the simple, bold lines of untutored pictures, weathervanes, and hooked rugs that decorated their studios. And the appeal of folk art went beyond the Ogunquit group: Charles Sheeler and Charles Demuth were among other painters attracted to it.

Sheeler encountered folk objects shortly after 1910, when he and Morton Schamberg rented a farmhouse in Bucks County, Pennsylvania. Encouraged by Henry Mercer, a collector and scholar of Pennsylvania folk art, Sheeler soon began to study the region's local art and architecture. He was particularly interested in both Pennsylvania German and Shaker design. Like other modern artists, his enthusiasm was not the result of primarily antiquarian interests, but rather contemporary aesthetic ones. "I don't like these things because they are old, " he said, "but in spite of it . . . I'd like them still better if they were made yesterday because then they would afford proof that the same kind of creative power is continuing."[17]

Sheeler soon started to collect folk objects; they began to appear frequently in his paintings. More important, however, he came to incorporate the geometric patterns and contours of Shaker and Pennsylvania German architecture and artifacts as design elements in his work. Already interested in the works of Cezanne, the Cubists, and the Fauves—which he had encountered in Paris in 1909—Sheeler interpreted folk art in a way that helped him "de-Europeanize" his paintings to eventually create, in his precisionist work, some of the most successful expressions of cubism in an American idiom. According to art critic Martin Friedman, "paradoxically, within the conservative, historical context of Doylestown Sheeler's painting began its modernist evolution. The localized, frugal quality of its architecture and crafts was absorbed in his art and never left it."[18]

Folk art was of interest to modern artists for more than aesthetic reasons, however. As an art of the past, folk art not only seemed to assert an indigenous tradition for American modern art, then seeking to defend itself against claims that it was only a copy of European styles, but also harkened back to the fondly and romantically remembered period before the forces of the machine and urbanism transfigured and unsettled American life. Created by preindustrial craftsmen in a pre-urban world, folk art came increasingly to be interpreted and valued by Americans as a symbol of the lifestyle and qualities they feared they were losing. Although these reactionary social interpretations would not be fully articulated until the late 1920s or early 1930s, they were already apparent by the mid-'20s, when American folk art began to be seen as a popular and even commercial commodity, to be bought and sold by art and antique dealers and collected by the public at large.

According to folk art scholar Beatrix Rumford, Isabel Carleton Wilde was the first dealer to recognize the commercial value of folk art, while modern art dealer Edith Gregor Halpert and museum curator Holger Cahill were most responsible for popularizing it as a collectible. Advertising in *The Magazine Antiques* in November 1926, Wilde announced that an "important exhibition of American Primitives including paintings on velvet and glass, portraits in oil, water colors, pastels, and tinsels" would be sold in her Cambridge, Massachusetts, antiques shop.[19] A few months earlier, during the summer of the same year, Edith Halpert, along with her husband and Holger Cahill, had visited the Ogunquit art school and, like the modern artists who summered there, recognized the appeal of the objects decorating the studio-cabins.[20] Shortly afterward—inspired by a recent trip to France, where she became aware of the value of supporting living artists and their

Edith Gregor Halpert in front of a painting by modern artist Charles Sheeler. Halpert is wearing a dress made of fabric designed by Sheeler. Photograph by Charles Sheeler. Courtesy of the Downtown Gallery Papers, Archives of American Art, Smithsonian Institution.

work—Halpert opened the Downtown Gallery in Greenwich Village, specializing in modern art. Soon after she also began to sell folk art.[21]

Both Isabel Wilde and Edith Halpert emphasized the aesthetic qualities of folk art. However, whereas Wilde sold her "American Primitives" within the context of her antiques shop, displayed among New England furniture and glass, Halpert accentuated the idea that folk art was "an intrinsically aesthetic expression" by selling it with modern art within the three-room exhibition space of the Downtown Gallery. It was in this fine art context that Halpert opened the American Folk Art Gallery in 1929, claiming that it was "the first of its kind in this country."[22] By categorically and physically juxtaposing folk art with fine art, Halpert continued, and profited from, the earlier fine art associations established by modern artist-collectors. While Isabel Wilde was forced out of the art and antiques business by the harsh economic forces of the Depression, Halpert's gallery survived—in large part because she had been able to develop and cultivate an aesthetic folk art market, which in the early 1930s even outsold her fine art offerings. Halpert "labored to create a market for folk art so that she would have the working capital to buy paintings from living [fine] artists who still were not selling well."[23] She referred to folk art as her "sugar daddy."

Halpert's success with folk art was primarily due to her ability to interest a number of wealthy and influential people in folk art through its fine art associations. Most notable of Halpert's patrons was Abby Aldrich Rockefeller, who began buying folk art in 1929. Between 1929 and the late 1930s, Rockefeller, who was also a major fine art collector, purchased dozens of American folk paintings and sculptures from Halpert, accumulating one of the most widely known and influential folk art collections of this century. Rockefeller's social position and financial resources suited Halpert's image of an ideal client—one who could afford not only to purchase numerous objects, but to display them in a way that enhanced their aesthetic, historical, and economic value—and through this presentation to popularize the genre. "We are opposed," Halpert wrote, "to the idea of selling individual items to persons who plan to use such pictures or sculpture as little household decorations. We feel strongly that this material is of great importance . . . and should be preserved now that it has been removed from parlors and attics."[24]

The significance of Rockefeller's patronage extended beyond the mere preservation of art or the financial security that such large-scale collecting afforded Halpert's Downtown Gallery. Within a few years after Rockefeller became a client of the American Folk Art Gallery, portions of her collection were loaned to major museums for public exhibition. These exhibitions, directly and indirectly engineered by Halpert and Holger Cahill, promoted in the popular mind an awareness of folk art as a valuable and significant object of American art. In 1931, Cahill borrowed approximately 20 objects owned by Rockefeller to display in his exhibition, "American Folk Sculpture," staged at the Newark Museum. In 1932, nearly every object exhibited in Cahill's monumental show, "American Folk Art, The Art of the Common Man," organized for the Museum of Modern Art, belonged to Abby Aldrich Rockefeller. And in 1935, Halpert was hired to direct the installation of a part of Rockefeller's folk art collection prominently displayed in the Ludwell-Paradise House in Williamsburg, Virginia.[25]

Halpert continued to pursue wealthy collectors—such as Harry du Pont and Edsel Ford—throughout the 1930s. Yet as early as 1931, with the official opening of the American Folk Art Gallery, Halpert had also begun to promote folk art to a wider and less affluent audience that included not only individuals, but also public institutions and art galleries across the nation.[26] Halpert's folk art correspondence throughout the decade reveals a steady flow of queries to and from private galleries, college museums, and historical societies regarding the sale or exhibition of folk art.[27] In reaching for a broader, more popular audience, Halpert came to emphasize in particular folk art's social and historical value as an American icon, a value that tied it to the popularity of the American Scene art movement.

Halpert's papers reveal numerous passages from her own writings, as well as those of others, expressing the importance of folk art as a symbolic representation of American patriotism. Quoting from statements by museum director John Cotton Dana, one set of Halpert's notes focuses on "the importance of artists as reporters, their special value not only in carrying on the cultural tradition, but also their unique contribution in creating a factual record and in reflecting the spirit of the times. 'Folk art is at once the best propaganda and the best social cement that democracy can have.'"[28]

Romantically presenting American folk art as a symbol of the historical forces that helped create and perpetuate America as a unique nation, Halpert wrote, "The people who came [to America] were mainly workers with no illusions about comfort and luxury. . . . They knew that a wilderness faced them, that physical hardships must be endured. . . . These communities created a classless society with common needs, common aspirations, and common philosophy." Espousing the same theme in another piece, Halpert wrote, "American Folk Art developed logically as an authentic expression of the community for the community, of the folk for the folk. It was the art of the masses rather than the classes—the art of a democracy where the aspirations of the many had a common denominator."[29] Yet while Halpert's marketing strategy hailed the importance of historical connection and kinship with tradition, her personal contacts with prospective buyers also continued to emphasize the aesthetic values of folk art. "There is no question but that this figurehead is very aged . . . [and] so fine as a work of art and is so definitely an old object of rare quality that I know you will be very enthusiastic when you see it."[30]

In 1937, Halpert began to expand her folk art marketing strategy to include yet another group: Hollywood celebrities. She tailored each letter to make it relevant to the potential buyer. Discovering that actress Irene Dunne was interested in early American carvings, for example, Halpert wrote, "It occurred to me that you would enjoy seeing our comprehensive collection. . . . I hope that when you are next in New York, you will come in to see this unique collection."[31] A few months later, she wrote to Clark Gable: "Our American Folk Art Gallery [has] a pair of portraits, one of which represents a gentleman of the 1820s dressed in all the elegance of the period. Several visitors remarked that this portrait bears a striking, if unflattering, resemblance to you in some of your costume parts. . . . While I am sending you this photograph merely as a souvenir, I shall be glad to quote prices. . . ."[32] An even greater effort to promote this market is indicated in a letter to Cecil B. De Mille: "I came across an article stating the ship figurehead carving is being revived in Hollywood and that you are planning to use several in your forthcoming picture 'The Buccaneer.' . . . You might be interested in learning that there are original figureheads available . . . in our American Folk Art Gallery. . . . I am enclosing a catalog of our present exhibition." Halpert's keen interest in encouraging folk art's popularity was stressed in the same letter: "I think it would be well worth your while to have a representative call to see some of the rare original objects which can be used in sets and will not cost as much as reproductions. This type of material will create a new type of publicity."[33]

While Halpert popularized folk art through her activities as an art dealer, Holger Cahill promoted the art form as a curator and writer. After arriving in New York in 1905 at the age of 18, Cahill studied aesthetics and art history at Columbia University and the New School for Social Research. By 1915 he had become well connected in the New York art world. A proponent of modernism who considered the National Academy "stifling" and "utterly dead,"[34] he was a friend of many prominent modernist artists and their supporters, such as Alfred Stieglitz, Georgia O'Keefe, John Sloan, Gaston Lachaise, Charles Sheeler, and Stuart Davis. Beginning in the early 1920s, Cahill worked with the Society of Independent Artists, publicizing their exhibitions.

The events that brought folk art to Cahill's attention began in 1921. In that year he met John Cotton Dana, director of the Newark Museum and a pioneering museologist. Committed to the museum as a public service institution, Dana was also fascinated with popular and industrial art. Somewhat contemptuous of the pretense of the established art scene, he often promoted the art of everyday life created by common people and even staged exhibitions of bathtubs and other plumbing fixtures.[35] Dana hired Cahill to publicize some of the Newark Museum exhibitions, and later to organize and curate them. Catholic in his aesthetic tastes, Dana backed Cahill in the face of objections from academicians when Cahill presented exhibitions of the work of the Society of

Independent Artists at Newark. In 1926 Dana reallocated $10,000 that had been given to the museum to buy Italian art, giving it instead to Cahill to purchase paintings by Max Weber, John Sloan, and other modern artists.[36] During the early 1920s, then, Cahill not only continued his interest in the new trends in fine art, but also began to develop a fascination with the aesthetic significance of common objects.

Connected to this fascination was Cahill's discovery of folk art. In the summer of 1922, while visiting Sweden, Norway, and Germany, Cahill found his attention arrested by the objects he discovered in numerous folk art museums. Shortly after he returned to the United States, his interest in folk art was piqued again when Dana showed him a mourning picture at his home in Vermont. Cahill had already heard about such objects in relationship to the Ogunquit artist colony, but it wasn't until 1926, when he actually visited Ogunquit with Edith Halpert, that he became captivated with folk art. Knowledgeable about Picasso's fascination with primitive objects and new movements like the "Blue Rider," Cahill discovered at Ogunquit a kind of object that he could appreciate in terms of both his developing commitment to everyday artifacts and his support for new American art.[37] In the next years Cahill would turn his considerable talents as a promoter to the publicizing of American folk art.

In 1930, 1931, and 1932, Cahill organized his first folk art exhibitions. Although these were not the first exhibitions of American folk art ever to be produced, in these shows—especially the remarkably popular and widely reviewed one staged in 1932—Cahill articulated and presented a vision of American folk art that would be a major influence in transforming folk art from the relatively unknown preoccupation of modern artists to a major popular phenomenon.

Cahill presented folk art in this 1932 catalogue in a way that Americans could, by this time, easily appreciate. Synthesizing the romantic folk art social dogma then current, he codified and established a popular aesthetic that fused folk meaning into fine art form. In doing this, of course, Cahill was using folk art in the same way as had the modern artists at Ogunquit. By 1932, however, the trends in the world of fine art had shifted and, with America in the depths of the Depression, folk art took on a new meaning.

According to art historian Matthew Baigell, "The first clear evidence of the movement known as the American Scene appeared during the exhibition season of 1931–32." A movement that sought to avoid foreign influences on American art and express the unique spirit and values of America, it encouraged indigenous artist traditions and the production of an art relevant to, and understandable by, all Americans. Hostile to the modernist reliance on personal sensibility as a dominant source of artistic motivation as well as to the abstracted forms of modernist art, the American Scene reflected an increased interest in realistic painting and in the "imperatives of place, politics, and history."[38] Unlike the modernist art of the previous decade, such an art could quickly capture popular support. And, ironically, although it was the early modernists who had first discovered and utilized folk art, folk art now began to receive widespread attention as an emblem of the American Scene. This wide popularity, however, was not based on folk art's modernist aesthetic associations but on its social and historical meanings, meanings that had existed in the 1920s but that Holger Cahill now emphasized and promoted in terms of the dilemmas of the early 1930s.

The exhibition "The Art of the Common Man" opened its doors in one of the gloomiest years in American history. Millions of unemployed industrial workers tramped the streets, farmers blocked highways to protest failed agriculture prices, and thousands of homeless people slept in doorways or on the ground. In the face of such overwhelming suffering, the undercurrents of uncertainty that had characterized the prosperous 1920s seemed relatively unimportant. Yet activities had begun in response to these undercurrents that would develop in the Depression years into prominent responses to the events of the time. In both the 1920s and 1930s these responses were often defensive and reactionary, resulting in political chauvinism, cultural isolationism, and emotional retreat. But it was through their expression in art—and not insignificantly through the popularization of folk art—that middle- and upper-class Americans discovered ways to cope with some of the dilemmas they confronted.

One of these responses was the popular cult of Americanism. Attempting to deny growing divisions in American society, many Americans in both decades retreated to a combative sense of oneness. Not only were Americans often hostile to all things foreign, but they glorified America and its founders and institutions. Admiration for American history and the American land approached an almost religious fervor as Americans lauded the virtues of democracy and the common man.

This self-conscious chauvinism expressed itself boldly in the rhetoric of the American Scene, the pronouncements of Edith Halpert, and especially in Holger Cahill's definition of American folk art. Said by Cahill to give "a living quality to the story of American beginnings," folk art was glorified as representative of the indigenous artistic heritage of a great democratic nation. Influenced by the environmentalist theories of art then prevalent, Holger Cahill's remarks in the mid-1930s that "art is a normal social growth . . . extremely sensitive to the environments created by human society" applied to his understandings not only of the American Scene but also of folk art.[39]

Thus American folk art was popularized as testimony to the fact that American life and activity were intrinsically artistic and beautiful, not in the contrived sense that informed European high art and its imitations, but in the simple way commonplace objects dignified the life of the American common man.

A second popular response during this period was to retreat into the past. The more uncomfortable the present became, the more Americans seemed to value the past, often in a substantially

Indian archer weathervane. N-219.79. Courtesy of the New York State Historical Association, Cooperstown.

Peaceable Kingdom by Edward Hicks. N-38.61. Courtesy of the New York State Historical Association, Cooperstown.

refashioned and romanticized form. The development of widespread interest in American folk art was but one example of this interest in the past. Thus, according to Holger Cahill and Edith Halpert, folk art was largely an historical phenomenon. Cahill's 1932 catalogue claimed that, fed by preindustrial craft traditions, folk art flourished in the 17th, 18th, and early 19th centuries. After the Civil War, with the advent of industrialization and urbanization, this art began to languish, and by the end of the century—according to Cahill—its production ceased.

A final way in which Americans sought to adjust to their contemporary discomforts was through their fascination with the romantic image of the common man. American modern artists in the

teens and 1920s had been partially drawn to the objects they identified as folk because interest in such "primitive" forms had already
been engendered by European modernism. During this period,
spurred by the development of modern techniques in anthropology, primitivism and interest in folk societies had become a fad
throughout the western world. The cult of primitivism helped
jaded sophisticates escape the pace and responsibilities of modern
life, allowing them to identify with those whose natural instincts,
it was believed, had not been corrupted by civilization. Primitivism
also romanticized and manipulated groups distinguished by their
non-European backgrounds or lower-class status.[40] In the 1930s
the popularity of the common man resulted in similar ends as
liberal and often well-meaning elites imposed their middle- and
upper-class visions and values on less socially powerful peoples.
Such an activity allowed folk art collectors of the time to affirm a
romantic, preindustrial image of labor, a vision that avoided confronting the harsh situation of the contemporary working man.
From the beginning, then, primitivism played an important role
in the discovery and definition of American folk art. Influenced
by the enthusiasm for so-called primitive art forms first evinced
by modern artists, Cahill popularized a vision of folk art in the
1930s that actually demeaned the very people it sought to affirm:
he branded the work of the American common man as "primitive
in the sense that it is the simple, unaffected and childlike expression of men and women . . . who did not even know that they were
producing art."[41]

Cahill's formulation of American folk art received the sanctification of official government approval at the end of the 1930s. Appointed in 1935 as the director of the Federal Arts Project, Cahill
was responsible for overseeing a program that supported
thousands of artists during the Depression. Cahill also oversaw the
creation of what became known as the Index of American Design,
"a collection of 22,000 pictures of objects of folk and popular
manufacture made before 1890."[42] The object of the index was to

Holger Cahill. Courtesy of the Photographs of Artists, Col. I and II, Archives of American Art, Smithsonian Institution.

give employment to artists, and to record material of historical significance as a basis for American design. It also was to create a record of the sources of these materials—but, as recent research by John Vlach has suggested, this second objective was abandoned midway through the project. Due to staffing changes and shifts in funding, ethnographic research on objects was often curtailed and omitted. Instead, the Index compilers came to be concerned with the aesthetic qualities of watercolor renderings and black-and-white photographs of craft objects. According to Vlach, "Cahill, who originally wanted the Index to be a work of scholarship, came to regard the art work as one of its best attributes"—but as the artistic quality of the Index rose, its documentary value faded.[43] Soon, without adequate contextual documentation, the Index became primarily a record of pretty objects, which could be easily interpreted in terms of the popular view of folk art presented by Cahill and Halpert.

Beginning in the late 1930s, sets of Index plates were shown in numerous public exhibitions across the country. These exhibitions were held not only in established museums, such as the Detroit Art Institute, but also in department stores such as Macy's and Marshall Field & Company, and they were enormously popular. A prime reason for their popularity was their folk art content, now presented as beautifully rendered art to a public who responded to such a presentation in the same way they responded to the folk art presented by Edith Halpert in her American Folk Art Gallery. Presentations such as those in Macy's and Marshall Field & Company not only increased the visibility and popularity of American folk art but emphasized its value as a popular, marketable commodity.

The incorporation of the idea of the folk into fine art as it occurred through the efforts of modern artists in the early years of the century, and the popularization of folk art through the work of Edith Halpert and Holger Cahill in the 1930s, was but a part of a larger cultural process of adjustment to a variety of social and historical forces. The meaning of folk art that resulted is as much a statement of culture as aesthetics. What must be recognized, however, is that this statement was fundamentally a conservative one, one that functioned to help many Americans avoid the implications of consuming social issues.

NOTES

With deepest gratitude, we dedicate this article to John Michael Vlach, whose commitment to the study of folk art and culture, combined with a generous and supportive nature, has provided us with invaluable guidance and encouragement.

1. "The Impact of the Concept of Culture on the Concept of Man," in Clifford Geertz, *The Interpretation of Cultures* (New York: Basic Books, 1973), pp. 33–54.
2. John Berger, *Ways of Seeing* (New York: Viking Press, 1973), chap. 1.
3. Constance Perin, "The Reception of New, Unusual and Difficult Art," in *The Prinzhorn Collection* (Champaign, Ill.: Krannert Art Museum, 1984), pp. 21–38.
4. Morse Peckham, *Man's Rage for Chaos: Biology, Behavior and the Arts* (New York & Philadelphia: Chilton Books, 1965), p. 314.
5. This process is the focus of T. J. Jackson Lears' book, *No Place of Grace: Antimodernism and the Transformation of American Culture 1880–1920* (New York: Pantheon, 1981). Although Lears' book does not focus directly on folk art, it considers many of the cultural forces that would contribute to folk art's discovery and popularity.
6. Information in this paragraph comes from Dorren A. Bolger, "Hamilton Easter Field and the Rise of Modern Art in America": (M.A. thesis, University of Delaware, Newark, 1973), pp. 5–6, 16, 19–20.
7. Ibid., pp. 39–40.
8. American Folk Art Writings, Box 99, Downtown Gallery Papers, Archives of American Art, Smithsonian Institution, Washington, D.C.
9. Daniel Robbins, "Statues to Sculpture: From the Nineties to the Thirties," in *200 Years of American Sculpture* (New York: David R. Godine, in association with the Whitney Museum of American Art, 1976), p. 114.
10. Ibid., p. 143.
11. Roberta K. Tarbell, "Direct Carving," in *Vanguard American Sculpture, 1913–1939*, by Joan M. Marter, Roberta K. Tarbell, and Jeffrey Wechsler (New Brunswick, N. J.: Rutgers University Art Gallery, 1979, p. 47.
12. Robbins, "Statues to Sculpture," p. 122.
13. Ibid., pp. 143–144.
14. Lincoln Kirstein, *Elie Nadelman* (New York: Eakins Press, 1973), p. 161.
15. Roberta K. Tarbell, "Figurative Interpretations of Vanguard Concepts," in *Vanguard American Sculpture, 1913–1939* , p. 32.
16. Elie Nadelman [notes], *Camera Work* 32 (October 1910).
17. Martin Friedman, *Charles Sheeler* (New York: Watson-Guptill, 1975), p. 20.
18. Ibid.
19. Beatrix T. Rumford, "Uncommon Art of the Common People: A Review of Trends in the Collecting and Exhibiting of American Folk Art," in eds., Ian M. G. Quimby

and Scott T. Swank, *Perspectives on American Folk Art* (New York: W. W. Norton for The Henry Francis du Pont Winterthur Museum, Winterthur, Del., 1980), pp. 19–21.

20. We are grateful to Diane Tepfer, an authority on Edith Gregor Halpert's Downtown Gallery, for her assistance with sources and her unfailing willingness to answer questions.

21. Avis Berman, "Pioneers in American Museums: Edith Halpert," *Museum News* (November/December 1975): 35.

22. American Folk Art Writings, Box 99, Downtown Gallery Papers, Archives of American Art, Smithsonsian Institution, Washington, D.C.

23. Berman, "Pioneers in American Museums," p. 36.

24. Letter, Edith Gregor Halpert to Walter Heil, April 14, 1937, Downtown Gallery Papers, Archives of American Art, Smithsonian Institution, Washington, D.C. All future references in this article to Halpert's correspondence belong to the same collection in the Archives of American Art.

25. Rumford, "Uncommon Art," p. 39.

26. American Folk Art Writings, Box 99, Downtown Gallery Papers, Archives of American Art, Smithsonian Institution, Washington, D. C.

27. Ibid.

28. American Folk Art Writings, Box 99, Downtown Gallery Papers, Archives of American Art, Smithsonian Institution, Washington, D. C.

29. Ibid.

30. Letter, Edith Gregor Halpert to Susan Higginson Nash, July 5, 1932.

31. Letter, Edith Gregor Halpert to Irene Dunne, February 27, 1937.

32. Letter, Edith Gregor Halpert to Clark Gable, May 20, 1937.

33. Letter, Edith Gregor Halpert to Cecil B. De Mille, September 29, 1937.

34. "The Reminiscences of Holger Cahill," *Columbia Oral History Collection* (New York: Columbia University, 1957), pp. 138–139.

35. John Michael Vlach, "Holger Cahill as Folklorist," *Journal of American Folklore* 98, no. 388 (1985): 153.

36. "The Reminiscences of Holger Cahill," p. 165.

37. Ibid., pp. 190–194.

38. Matthew Baigell, *The American Scene: American Painting of the 1930s* (New York: Praeger, 1974), p. 18.

39. Holger Cahill, *New Horizons in American Art* (New York: Museum of Modern Art, 1936), p. 9.

40. The portrayal of black Americans as primitives and the social implications of that portrayal has been studied by Eugene Metcalf in 33 "Black Art, Folk Art and Social Control," *Winterthur Portfolio* 18 (1983): 271–289.

41. Holger Cahill, *American Folk Art: The Art of the Common Man in America, 1750–1900* (New York: Museum of Modern Art, 1932), p. 5.

42. John Michael Vlach, "The Index of American Design: From Reference Tool to Shopper's Guide." (Paper presented to the Annual Meeting of the American Folklore Society, Albuquerque, October 1987).

43. Ibid.

When We Were Good:
The Folk Revival

❧ ROBERT CANTWELL ❧

I NEED a steamshovel mama, to keep away the dead!" Bob Dylan swore in 1965, having personally terminated the popular folk song revival, some thought, by picking up an electric guitar and sending his message over the horizon with it. "I need a dump truck mama, to unload my head. . . ."[1]

Having shared and brought to light so much of the experience of his generation, perhaps Dylan was remembering an evening in the parlor back in Hibbing, Minnesota, in front of the new television set, where in films supplied by the Department of the Army a man with a surgical mask, operating a bulldozer, was moving a naked trash-heap of human corpses into an open pit. Or it may have been the sudden rising of a momentary sun over Bikini Atoll, disemboweling the sky in membraneous sheets of dust and light and summoning out of the earth a pillar of smoke and steam in which the Pacific tried to leap out of itself. Or maybe he was remembering a dim Senate committee room where bespectacled men in front of microphones shouted at one another with anger and indignation, or gravely intoned a refusal to answer on the strange "grounds" that their answer might "tend to incriminate" them. No wonder he saw history, on that same record album, as the work of a fancy promoter, who, when asked whether he could produce "the next world war," says, "yes, I think it can be very *easily* done!—just put some bleachers out in the sun" and have it out on the old Mississippi Delta highway, "Highway Sixty-One."[2]

If you were born into the white middle-class between roughly

167

1941 and 1950, you grew up in a reality perplexingly divided by the intermingling of an old world and a new. Obscurely taking shape around you, of a definite order and texture, was an environment of new neighborhoods, new schools, new businesses, new forms of recreation and entertainment, new technologies, even of new ways of thinking, which in the course of the 1950s would virtually efface the older world in which your parents had grown up. Yet you had been born soon enough to take the lingering traces of an earlier way of life, though uncomprehendingly, into your own nature.

You may have been reared, for example, much as your parents had, in a slightly more rigorous style than that shortly to be advocated by Dr. Benjamin Spock. And you absorbed, as you grew to awareness, your parents' almost unlimited hopes for you—for to them, who had grown up in depression and war, the relatively prosperous and tranquil life of postwar America was the end of the rainbow, a new dispensation in which anything was possible. Very likely you saw yourself growing up to be a doctor or lawyer, scientist or engineer, teacher, nurse, or mother (sexual discrimination being still quite marked)—all careers that were seen as models of success. And yet in this vision of the future there was a lingering note of caution, even of dread, so that although quite glamorous it had very little of the unconventional in it, and none of the revolutionary.

You probably attended, too, an overcrowded public school—typically a building built shortly before the First World War to which a new wing had recently been added to accommodate the burgeoning school-age population—and you may have had to share a desk with another student. In addition to the normal fire and tornado drills, you also had bomb drills, during which you climbed under your desk in order to shelter yourself from the imagined explosion of an atomic bomb: "first there's a flash of light. . . ."

That such a thing might come, and soon, was one of the axioms of daily life; you had seen the atomic explosion on the television, which had come into your parlor around 1952 or 1953. On television, in the Saturday movie matinees, in the immediate memory of parents and teachers—all around you was evidence of the major global catastrophe that had recently spent itself. There was, moreover, a dark colossus, the Soviet Union, and an insidious influence, the Communist party, which in some obscure way were connected to one another, were foreign in a colorless, unsavory way, and were dedicated, you were taught, to conquering us from above, with a rain of bombs, or from within, through an unexplained but picturesque technique called "brainwashing." It is not inconceivable, in fact, that one of your neighbors was actually digging a fallout shelter in his backyard.

Your house in the suburbs, with its new television set, your two-car garage with gleaming, garish cars: these were trophies of the enthusiastic consumerism of the postwar period, the uninhibited reaching after a dream long deferred by wartime deprivations. Being widely shared and widely promulgated, and largely mass-produced, that dream brought with it a certain uniformity on the social landscape. To grasp that dream probably required the principal wage-earner in your family, most likely your father, to surrender to the tightly regimented, highly competitive, and bureaucratic organization of the newly efficient, even somewhat militarized, postwar American business establishment.

Bureaucratization, conformity, and consumerism did not perhaps touch you in the same way as they touched your parents; nevertheless they touched you. You tended, for example, to identify yourself with children your own age, who were more or less like yourself, socially and culturally, and to think of the more or less uniform world of children in which you lived as the norm. You were not, in other words, much acquainted in your immediate experience with human variety, and may have been inclined, or even taught, to look upon difference with suspicion. Your nuclear family, bivouacked in the suburbs with other families more or less like yourselves, had effectively reduced the generational spectrum to a bipolar relationship between parent and child, while the new consolidated public school you attended was strictly stratified by grade—and in some schools even more scrupulously by less tangible standards, such as "aptitude." In fact, as you advanced in school you were subject to evermore elaborate forms of quantitative evaluation to distinguish you from your fellows—so difficult to distinguish in other ways—a process of IQ tests, achievement tests, aptitude tests, and the like, whose crowning glory was the new Scholastic Aptitude Test, with its inexorable power to define, delimit, and foreclose.

At the same time, though, you were granted intimations of a variegated and enigmatic world beyond the suburban street, which occasionally disturbed the otherwise uniform surface of social reality. There were the desks in the old school building, for example, with their inkwells, and, of course, the schoolteachers, with their old-fashioned discipline. There were the old houses on Main Street, too, as well as Main Street itself, whose deterioration would not be complete until business had moved entirely out to the shopping mall. Perhaps you had European-born grandparents, still in their stuffy East Side flat or on the farm; or knew a "colored man," born in Mississippi, who came to mow the lawn, and played the harmonica; or had a schoolmate with a southern accent, whose father had come from Kentucky to work at the foundry or the auto plant—and who, to your amazement, brought a giant flat-top guitar to the fifth-grade talent show, where he played and sang in a piping voice "Your Cheatin' Heart."

Similarly disquieting, perhaps, and fascinating, was the gang of young toughs from the other side of town, slightly older perhaps— the "hoods" or "greasers" you called them—who wore, with their long hair and sideburns, the uniform of the motorcyclist: black leather jackets with many zippers and pockets, garrison belts, faded blue jeans, and black engineer boots with silver buckles.

If these figures in the remoter parts of the social landscape had attracted your attention, it was perhaps because of their certain strange resonance with more strictly imaginary realms of your cultural life: realms whose romantic texture and tensile strength made your own world seem chimerical by comparison. Wild Bill Hickok, the Lone Ranger, the Cisco Kid, Wyatt Earp, and a hundred other Western heroes galloped across television and movie screens on Saturday mornings and afternoons; frontiersmen Mike Fink and Davy Crockett conquered the wilderness in weekly after-dinner episodes; Ichabod Crane, Johnny Appleseed, Pecos Bill, and other folk legends came to life again in Disney's animated cartoons. Very likely in reading class you learned of frontier childhoods in Laura Ingalls Wilder's *Little House* books, which were republished in a new edition illustrated by Garth Williams in 1953. In music class you may have sung "Cindy" and "She'll Be Comin' 'round the Mountain" and other folk songs.[3] You may have sung folk songs at summer camp, too, where your college-age counselor had a banjo, or at scout camp, where you practiced the arts of wilderness survival and learned Indian lore. Or you may have heard the special series of folk song recordings issued by the Children's Record Guild, Young People's Records, and other companies, and accompanied by pictures and narratives of such events as the completion of the transcontinental railroad.[4] In short, you had been the beneficiary, in school and at home, of cultural traditions both learned and popular which had already enjoyed a long life in America. During the epoch of your childhood, these traditions were being hastily quarried out of literature and the arts to supply swelling public school enrollments, a swiftly expanding new commercial market, the youth market, and capacious new media such as television and the microgroove record.

The social development which would most influence your adolescence, and most color the attitudes with which you approached adulthood, was the slow invasion, as if by a migrating people, of the huge numbers of children born into the swiftly suburbanizing society after 1946. In the period immediately after the war, the birthrate increased by a million; after a peak in 1957 postwar births eventually accounted for roughly one-third of the total population: 76 million people.[5] This was the "baby boom," which saturated the marketplace with its buying power and popular culture with its image. It created a broad and dynamic consumer group whom the commercial establishment has followed with eager solicitousness through each stage in its life cycle literally to the present moment.

The baby boomers were consumers and through their consumption grew to an awareness of themselves as a generation. Perhaps the Mouseketeers, the baby-boom television confirmation class, defined its temporal boundaries: Karen, the youngest Mouseketeer, was about eight, and Bobby, the eldest, 18. Careful market research, no doubt, had fixed these limits. The evolution of this generation lasted roughly 20 years, from the mid-1950s to the mid-1970s, in which middle-class children enjoyed a degree of imaginative independence from the parent culture. This was a period that began in front of the television set, and moved to the sanctuary of the adolescent child's private bedroom with its radio, phonograph, and perhaps a telephone, into the college years of dramatically augmented personal and intellectual freedom. Some of this generation entered a period of prolonged economic and social experimentation secured initially through communal and subsistence living, alternative crafts and trades, which gave us the "hippie" and other countercultural movements.

Yet if you had been born during the war, you were not, strictly speaking, a baby-boomer, for your rearing, your nurture, and your imaginative life were grounded in a society not yet dominated by the needs and desires of the young. Nevertheless you *were* young; and the generation coming up swiftly behind you came increasingly to shape the culture that you sought to embrace and in which you hoped to find yourself reflected. The parent generation came increasingly, though imprecisely, to identify you with these baby-boomers. Inevitably, though perhaps uneasily, your imaginative life and your social identity came to mingle with theirs.

Cultural traditions, and the social classes, communities, and families that carry them on, do not disperse themselves lineally across the generations, nor do cultural influences confine themselves within the classes, communities, and families that generate them. What may have been, 30 years ago, the cultural advantages of monied classes are now widely enjoyed by the middle classes; what was a middle-class movement 20 years ago may now be the affectation of young college bohemians. A child may, on account of an elder sibling's (or uncle's or cousin's) influence, seem out of step with peers, a throwback to the last decade; one may be, on account of influences that will be detected only in retrospect, a pioneer in a movement yet to be. Nevertheless, we can perhaps distinguish, with admitted imprecision, a transitional group—the group whose formative years we have just sketched—whose most pressing concern in the years of its individual and collective adolescence and young adulthood was to reconcile morally and imaginatively, the ideals, images, and hopes that parents had bestowed with the promise of a new society.

The postwar "folk revival" was an attempt at such a reconciliation. Between roughly 1958, when the Kingston Trio recorded the Appalachian murder ballad, "Tom Dooley," which sold nearly four million discs, and 1964, when the Beatles and other British rock groups began to dominate American popular music, folk songs—as well as original songs conceived and performed as folk songs—enjoyed an unprecedented commercial popularity. Sung by young folk-song revivalists such as Bob Dylan, Joan Baez, Peter, Paul and Mary, and literally hundreds of others, these songs inspired thousands of young middle-class men and women to learn folk music, to accompany themselves on folk instruments, particularly the guitar and banjo, to search out and lionize authentic folk musicians, and finally to dress, groom, speak, comport themselves, and even to think in ways suggestive of the rural, ethnic, proletarian and other marginal cultures to whom folk song was supposed to belong.

The young people who carried the folk revival—whom

folklorist Alan Lomax called, by analogy to "beatniks," the "folkniks"[6]—were a discrete people, a kind of Jewry, contained by a host society but generating, through their own commercial power, a culture of their own, in a marketplace characterized by the effort to redeem, at first innocently and awkwardly, but in time with all sophistication and deliberation, the cultural promise of their own imaginative education. This was not yet the "counterculture" of the mid- to late 1960s, though in a few years the counterculture would grow in the economic and social territory the folkniks had cleared. The audience the folk revival attracted, the audience that assembled around Bob Dylan after his conversion to electric instruments and the hybrid "folk-rock" he originated, though perhaps only a few years younger than Dylan himself, constituted the "rock culture" with which we now identify the late 1960s.

No one should be surprised that the folkniks' imaginations had been shaped by their many cultural advantages. Among these was, of course, education itself, the importance of which had been consistently emphasized at home. The unintended consequence of this emphasis was that certain young idealists—perhaps those whose parents had more impressed them with the importance of a college education—were inclined to take ideas of revolutionary philosophers, poets, and writers of Europe and America seriously—though the effects upon attitudes and values tended to be disruptive, since postwar society showed little of the influence of, say, Marx or Nietzsche. For once in college, the folkniks encountered in others like themselves a new boldness—even a subtle nonconformity—a willingness, for example, to undertake academic majors in art, philosophy, or literature rather than more careerist programs in the social or natural sciences. Allied to the interest in folk music, moreover, was an interest in intriguing new fashions of uncertain origin: young women with long, natural hair wore peasant skirts and handcrafted sandals and barrettes; young men whose hair had been clipped by their girlfriends, not by the barber, sported sideburns or beards, and wore workshirts and handcrafted leather belts with brass buckles. These had come from the galleries and import shops of bohemian enclaves such as Greenwich Village, or from summer watering spots and artists' colonies such as Woodstock, Provincetown, and Martha's Vineyard: sites of the urban left-wing folksong movement, which would lend its songs, styles, and even some of its political ideas to the folk revival.

With assent of their peers and the sanction of the college environment, the folkniks slowly began to conceive the idea that the parent generation had gravely mismanaged the world. For set cruelly against the high expectations for the future which parents had inculcated, and against the richness and color of the promised society, was a nagging fear that the future might at any moment be suddenly taken away, or that failure to measure up to some arbitrary standard would close off access to it. Through the glory with which the world had been invested ran a thick streak of the sinister. And, in case anyone had forgotten about the Bomb, the Cuban missile crisis of 1962 refreshed the national memory and filled the atmosphere with the mood of apocalypse.

In such an atmosphere it seemed essential to take matters into one's own hands—after all, young people seemed to fill the field of vision; they had become a power. This was an urgent and intoxicating idea, but it differed from the revolutionary ideas of the counterculture, which would shortly bury the folk revival, in one important respect: the folkniks' generation sought, or tacitly believed in, until deep political and social polarizations betrayed that belief, the blessing of the parent generation—for folkniks' high purposes were precisely the return on the investment the parents had made in their children. By the late 1950s stirrings of activism, largely dormant since the 1930s, now underwritten by a cautious and watchful confidence in its fundamental compatibility with the ideals and values that class and education had instilled, began to reappear on college campuses: politically in organizations such as the Student Peace Union, culturally in a new enthusiasm for folk music. These two movements were united in the goal of bringing about the world the parent culture had implicitly promised—one by removing the most conspicuous impediment to it, the Bomb, and the other by figuring forth the culture in which a war- and weapon-liberated people might live—a culture rooted in prewar America, one that could not be suburbanized out of existence.

Thus the folk revival was neither reactionary nor revolutionary, though it borrowed the signs of other such movements and subcultures to express its sense of difference from the parent culture. It was, instead, conservative, or more precisely, restorative, a kind of cultural patriotism dedicated to picking up the threads of a common legacy that the parent generation had either denied or forgotten, and weaving them into the present. In spite of appearances, this was the dream of children fundamentally obedient, of good kids: underneath the "cultivated, ultimately clean-cut unkemptness" of the folk revivalist, wrote Paul Nelson, "there beat the heart not of a ramblin' gamblin' hobo, but of a Boy Scout."[7]

The groundwork of the folk revival had been laid in the 1950s by one of the most remarkable entrepreneurial successes in the youth market, rock-and-roll—remarkable because of its apparently obscure sociocultural origins. Rock-and-roll had its roots sometime in the 1940s, when white performers began "covering" black rhythm-and-blues recordings normally distributed only within the black community. But when black "jump" blues was covered in Memphis, beginning in 1954, by young, white, working-class southerners—the best known was, of course, Elvis Presley—rock-and-roll found its audience. This music was unquestionably a kind of folk music, with roots extending deeply into the black and white folk cultures of the South. Both the ever-more portable radio and 45-rpm discs made the music readily available to the young and a constant accompaniment to their lives.

The inexpensive and virtually indestructible 45-rpm rockabilly disc was in the weeks of its currency a kind of cryptogram that could be deciphered—much to the dismay of parents—by constant repetition. If its message seemed an urgent one, one that established itself only by increments in a child's understanding, it was because at the moment of sexual awakening, images of exotic sexual culture were for the space of a few moments borne in upon the listener through the rhythms of the jukejoint and barrelhouse. These images—the levee and the boondocks, where abandoned lovers take up lodgings at the end of Lonely Street, stand at their windows and moan, or sneak into one another's houses like dogs— came in trappings that disarmed the teenagers' resistance: a straining vocality, sinewy with sexual tension, of young, white men.[8] The arm languidly pointing, the sneer, the sideburns, the sidelong grin, the sexual footwork: Presley's image was the pattern for a thousand pubescent boys lip-synching before their bedroom mirrors with their first cheap guitars. What did the 12- or 14-year-old know of the idiom and manners of the frankly erotic, unsentimental, and passionate black underworld of New Orleans or Memphis? Nothing. But rockabilly music, like the thief who doffs his clothes to baffle the guard dog, had made it a part of the boys' life.

The authentic rockabilly sound swiftly declined in the face of massive commercialization, marketing, and sex scandals, and, most of all, the disappearance of the authentic performers: Presley was drafted into the Army; Carl Perkins seriously injured in an auto accident; Chuck Berry and Jerry Lee Lewis disgraced; Buddy Holly, Eddie Cochran, and Gene Vincent killed. So sweeping was the catastrophe one can almost imagine that some sinister, quasi-official conspiracy was behind it. A vacuum in popular music had opened: and a broad sector of the middle-class young turned, at that moment, to a music that ingeniously sublimated already awakened musical proclivities on behalf of a new and more scrupulous social self-awareness.

Like the rockabilly combos, the Kingston Trio, whose "Tom Dooley" is usually regarded as the starting bell of the folk revival, was a string band of young white men singing in untrained natural voices, accompanying themselves with open chords on at least one freely resonating acoustic guitar—a deposit from traditional country music. Though it did not have the rhythmic drive of rockabilly, the music of the Kingston Trio (and of the trio's many imitators, such as the Cumberland Three, the Chad Mitchell Trio, and the Highwaymen) was nevertheless essentially aural, amateur, and traditional—what would loosely be called "folk" music—and hence independently reproducible, theoretically by any untrained person. "Tom Dooley," moreover, told a story, not frankly sexual but darkly so, of murder and execution, furnished like a folktale with vivid concretions—the knife, the white oak tree, a man called Grayson—sung in a cloaked, melancholy voice, putatively by a hapless mountaineer with an Irish name, and accompanied by a banjo that spoke obscurely of the frontier.

But the Kingston Trio's music was delivered with an articulation and phrasing perceptibly bookish, in musical settings wholesomely pianistic; with their colorful short-sleeved ivy-league shirts, close-cropped hair, their easy drollery and unambiguous enthusiasm, this West Coast group was manifestly collegiate. The Kingston Trio seemed to be on spring break somewhere on the beach. Even so, in the music of this group, underneath the gleam of sporty arrangements and expensive harmonies, there was something imperfectly beckoning; though unapologetically commercial, the trio had struck a primitive note.

"Tom Dooley" commemorated the murder of Laura Foster of Wilkes County, North Carolina, by a Civil War veteran, Tom Dula, and his co-conspirator and lover, Annie Melton. Dula was convicted and hung in 1868. Even New York newspapers covered Dula's trial, and at least one of the ballads about him, or attributed to him, may have been composed by a journalist named Thomas Land. It entered tradition, in any case, in Tennessee and North Carolina, where in 1938 Frank Proffitt, an ingenuous mountaineer from Pick Britches Valley, Tennessee, sang it for a folksinger-

The Kingston Trio on Capitol Records. Private collections. Photo: John Miller Documents.

collector, Frank Warner.[9] Now Proffitt, whose grandparents had
been personally acquainted both with the murderer and his victim,
had first heard "Tom Dooley" from his father, who had taught it
to him on a homemade banjo. Warner, who worked for the YMCA
in New York, sang the song in his lectures and concerts for 20
years, and taught it to folklorist Alan Lomax, who printed it without the third stanza in his book *Folk Song U.S.A.* in 1947.[10] This
was where Dave Guard, of the Kingston Trio, discovered the song;
Lomax's version somewhat simplified the detailed narratives in
the available traditional texts in favor of an evocative lyricism
reminiscent of folk songs sung in school, while Ruth Seeger's
sturdy musical arrangement dispelled what to the school-trained
ear are the melodic vagaries of the traditional Appalachian singing
style.

Dave Guard had first been inspired to undertake the banjo in
1954, after attending a performance by Pete Seeger in Palo Alto,
where Guard was a student (a very young Joan Baez was also in
attendance with her parents).[11] Guard even learned his banjo technique from Seeger's little book, *How to Play the 5-String Banjo.*[12] He
formed a band and named it "The Kingston Trio" to associate it
with the calypso songs such as "Jamaica Farewell," recently popularized by Harry Belafonte.[13]

From the immediate background of the Kingston Trio's "Tom
Dooley," one might vaguely surmise that the song had not sprung
full-blown out of a record promoter's imagination in 1958: that it
had a complex lineage of scholarly, entrepreneurial, musical,
theatrical, and political activity of fairly long standing and thor-
oughly authentic origins. The Kingston Trio, in fact, had not been
the first to record "Tom Dooley"; G. B. Grayson, a blind fiddler
from Mountain City, Tennessee, and a descendant of the "Grayson" who had arrested the murderer, had recorded the song for
Victor Records in the 1920s, along with "Handsome Molly," "Little
Maggie," and other songs that would become staples of the folk
revival.[14]

It is all very well to locate the commercial folk revival in the youth culture of postwar America. Nevertheless, one has only to scratch the surface of "Tom Dooley," as thousands of its young admirers did, to discover that in fact youth culture of the late 1950s had suddenly been intersected by a rich and energetic tradition of folk song scholarship, collection, and performance extending back at least into the regional festivals, folk dance societies, and outing clubs of the 1920s. In the larger historical perspective, this tradition belonged to a particular family of theatrical, literary and musical representations of folk song and folk culture which had begun in America on the minstrel stage—as far back as the 1830s, when T. D. Rice introduced the Negro Stableman's torturous jig he called "Jump Jim Crow."

In 1950, the Weavers' "Good Night, Irene," learned from the great black songster Huddie Ledbetter (whom John and Alan Lomax had brought from a Louisiana penitentiary to New York in 1934), was the year's most popular song. The Weavers made Leadbelly's "Kisses Sweeter Than Wine" a hit as well, and Woody Guthrie's dustbowl anthem, "So Long, It's Been Good to Know Ya," along with the South African "Wimoweh" and the Appalachian "On Top of Old Smoky." But the Weavers' career was soon terminated by McCarthyism and show-business blacklisting, which drove folk singing underground for most of the decade. It was precisely this momentary obscurity, the effect of the association of folk song with the political Left forged in the 1930s, which opened the immense aural and written resources of folk song and folk singing to the young and made it, by virtue of their independent recovery of it, their own. When folk song reemerged into the light of popular culture in 1958—its ideological connections having been largely suppressed, abandoned, forgotten, or lost—it welled up with all the freshness and vitality of a renewed cultural symbol eager for a rearticulation of itself.

The immediate foreground of "Tom Dooley" may suggest what fertile cultural ground was to be discovered in the folk tradition.

Inspired by the scholarly *Folkways Anthology of American Folk Music*, which reissued in 1953 folk songs recorded commercially in the 1920s, young folk song enthusiast Ralph Rinzler journeyed to North Carolina to record the elderly banjoist and singer Tom Ashley, who had been an early associate of G. B. Grayson on the medicine show circuit.[15] Ashley's "Coo Coo Bird," a mountain song with medieval English roots, had become a folk revival standard. Ashley introduced Rinzler to Doc Watson, a blind rockabilly guitarist living nearby. When Watson learned of Rinzler's interest in folk song, he picked up a banjo and sang a version of "Tom Dooley" that was *not* the Kingston Trio's popular version. This "new" version—as well as the whole story of the murder—had been in Watson's family for generations: his great-grandmother, Betsy Tripplett Watson, had been at Annie Melton's deathbed to hear her confession. Yet Rinzler needn't have traveled far to find the version he knew from the Kingston Trio: Frank Proffitt lived a few minutes down the road.

Tom Ashley and Frank Proffitt—along with other rediscovered mountain banjoists such as Hobart Smith and Roscoe Holcomb, and country bluesmen such as Mississippi John Hurt and Son House—returned with the encouragement of enterprising revivalists like Rinzler to university concert halls, coffee house circuits, and commercial festivals at Newport, Philadelphia, Chicago, and Monterey to play the songs and tunes they had recorded commercially 35 or 40 years earlier. A newly discovered Doc Watson, an expert singer and instrumentalist intimately acquainted with traditional mountain music, became one of the titans of the folk revival. Ralph Rinzler, after conducting fieldwork for the Newport Folk Foundation on Cape Breton and among the Cajuns of Louisiana, went on to become the director of the Smithsonian Institution's Festival of American Folklife first held in 1967 on the National Mall.[16]

Many revivalists were compelled, like Rinzler, to follow the circuitous trail of folk songs and folk singers into the Appalachian Mountains or as far as the Mississippi Delta. But many more found

irresistible the anomalies in the musical sound itself, most conspicuous of which, in the Kingston Trio's music, was Dave Guard's
banjo. This was an oddly elongated variant of its 19th-century
original, with a tuning peg fixed halfway up a neck to which three
extra frets had been added—an innovation Pete Seeger made in
1944.[17] The cultural history of the banjo was a complete enigma:
it was abandoned by black culture, which had reconstructed it
from an African original, abandoned by the Gilded Age parlor
society in which it had had a brief vogue, abandoned by jazz as jazz
moved uptown. The banjo was the instrument that had been left
behind. As minstrelsy's signature instrument, the banjo suggested
the spartan and adventurous spirit of the itinerant player or circus
roustabout, uncompromised by ties to family, community, or society; to play it was a simple and honest, even a homely occupation,
a kind of trade, like carpentry, or a craft, like spinning. To the
young imagination that looked across the landscape of postwar
society then, and found not a single pathway to its liking, the banjo
was a gate, and it had just swung open.

For many, of course, the amateur singing of folk songs was
simply a dormitory pastime, which after graduation went the way
that tarot cards or love beads would a few years later. But often,
as Carl Sandburg wrote in his *American Songbag* of 1927, "a song
is a role. The singer acts a part. . . . There is something authentic
about any person's way of giving a song which has been known,
lived with and loved, for many years, by the singer."[18] To study a
song, remarked Israel Young, proprietor of MacDougal Street's
Folklore Center in Greenwich Village, "makes a student feel allied
to it. It enables a girl who grew up surrounded by the best of
everything to sing with some conviction the kinds of blues and
spirituals that, theoretically, could be sung honestly only by a pris-
oner on a Southern chain gang."[19] To this an especially sensitive
observer of the folk revival, Susan Montgomery, added:

> Why American college students should want to express the ideas
> and emotions of the downtrodden and the heartbroken, of garage
> mechanics and millworkers and miners and backwoods farmers, is

in itself an interesting question. But there is certainly good reason for students today to find the world brutal and threatening, and one suspects that when they sing about the burdens and sorrows of the Negro, for example, they are singing out of their own state of mind as well.[20]

"Many of them," Montgomery observed of the early folk song revivalists,

> in some small detail of their appearance, looked ever so slightly beat. The badge of identity was sometimes a beard, worn as if in defiance of its owner's Shetland sweater or expensively tailored Madras shorts, or a workman's blue shirt tucked carelessly into faded jeans. Or a girl might go in for wrought-iron jewelry or long straight hair or a Mexican cotton skirt or handsome hand-crafted leather sandals.

Folk music, she understood, had "come to represent a slight loosening of the inhibitions, a tentative step in the direction of the open road, the knapsack, the hostel."[21] By 1965, Paul Nelson noted, the folk singer's persona had assumed a loosely conventional form, that of the "casually road-weary" traveler in jeans and boots or peasant frocks, unclipped hair, speaking a pidgin idiom neither South nor West but vaguely regional and proletarian and, with a touch of the library in it, "highly humane."[22]

John Cohen, a Yale graduate who became one of the leaders in the revival of old-time string-band music, remarked the "intensity" arising "from the struggle with forces in the music itself—which become as real as any other problem of life."[23] Many students abandoned their studies, and their professional careers with them, in response to those forces: to the demands of the bluegrass banjo style or the blues guitar. These were "bedeviled people," Montgomery concluded, "who should be counted among the casualties of contemporary American life."[24] One such casualty was Cohen himself, a photographer by vocation; he joined with Tom Paley, a City College old-time music enthusiast, and Mike Seeger, Pete's younger half-brother, to form the pioneer revivalist string band, the New Lost City Ramblers. Setting the pattern for the hundreds of amateur bands that followed their example, the New Lost City Ramblers offered concerts of old-time music painstakingly reconstructed from commercial discs recorded in the 1920s by such bands as Charlie Poole and the North Carolina Ramblers, Gid Tanner and His Skillet Lickers, and J. E. Mainer's Mountaineers. In addition to their expert musicianship, arcane scholarship, and a demeanor sober enough for the recital hall, the New Lost City Ramblers presented themselves like railroad stationmasters or telegraph operators of 1885, in vests, shirtsleeves and neckties, and posed for an album cover photograph, its surface artificially mottled and cracked, with the blank faces and straight spines of a small-town portrait studio of the last century.

But no career better embodies the folk revival than that of Bob Dylan, whose audacious autometamorphosis sanctioned and consolidated the movement already abroad in youth culture. Born Robert Zimmerman in 1941, he grew up in working-class, predominantly Catholic, Hibbing, Minnesota, the son of a Jewish hardware merchant. As his biographer, Anthony Scaduto, points out, Zimmerman was subject to all the influences that marked the period for people his age: films such as *Blackboard Jungle* with its theme song "Rock Around the Clock," a rhythm-and-blues cover by Bill Haley and the Comets; James Dean's *Rebel Without a Cause* and *East of Eden*; and the rock-and-roll shouter Little Richard, the first to bring the emotional energy of black gospel singing uncompromisingly into secular music.[25] Having heard and imitated honky-tonk singer Hank Williams on the radio, however, as well as blues singers such as Muddy Waters and Howlin' Wolf broadcast from Little Rock, Zimmerman had a deeper understanding of the roots of rock-and-roll, perhaps, than suburban youths who first encountered it in Elvis Presley.

It is certain in any case that life on the Mesabi Iron Range in Hibbing, in a community of open-pit miners, differed from life in Great Neck. In order to find acceptance among his schoolmates, Zimmerman strove to efface his Rotarian domestic background;

by the time he was 16, he was riding with the local "greasers" and fronting a rock-and-roll band at the piano, struggling to sound like Little Richard. When in September 1959 he pledged the Jewish fraternity at the University of Minnesota, Zimmerman had abandoned his leather jacket and jeans for the collegiate button-down shirt, chinos, and white bucks of the day. In a matter of months, however, having encountered the beatniks and folk singers in Dinkytown, Minneapolis's riverfront bohemia, and read Woody Guthrie's autobiography *Bound for Glory*, he had become Bob Dylan. To anyone who asked, Dylan claimed to be an orphan reared in Oklahoma, or in Gallup, or Sioux Falls, a former pianist for Bobby Vee, a circus hand, carny, railroad bum, streetsinger. But ultimately he was the youth in the fleece-lined jacket and corduroy cap who, sizing up his new audience from the cover of his first record album like a suitor who thinks he may be in love, had dared to offer himself, after his pilgrimage to Woody Guthrie's bedside, as the lad upon whom Guthrie's mantle would—and did—fall. Who Bob Dylan was was anybody's guess; but Columbia's high-fidelity microgrooves brought his callow voice, wretchedly overwrought, his stagey Panhandle dialect, his untutored guitar and harmonica—all his gallant fraudulence—into dormitory rooms with shocking immediacy. And when, in the spoken preface to his shattering "Baby Let Me Follow You Down," he waggishly reported that he had learned the song from one "Rick Von Schmidt," a "blues guitar player" from Cambridge, who he had "met one day in the green pastures of . . . ah . . . Harvard University," the folk revival knew it had found one of its own.

To the parent generation, the folk revivalist could scarcely be distinguished, on the one hand, from the motorcyclists and street gangs of the 1950s, whose crypto-fascist style was rooted in postwar social dislocations, or, on the other, from the beatniks, the jazz-centered subculture of urban bohemians who had modeled themselves loosely on the life of the Left Bank of Paris, finding a metaphor for the conduct of an awakened mind in postwar consumer America in the French underground resistance to the official culture of wartime France.

In fact, as Dylan's career illustrates, the folk revivalists *had* adapted, early on, these styles of youthful dissent, the one belonging to the working class and the other largely to the wealthy, educated, and well-traveled—but not without subtle displacements and sublimations. The aggressive black leather and silver chains of the motorcycle cowboy became a dry-goods costume of coarse textures and natural hues, strongly influenced by Clint Eastwood, James Arness, and other "adult" television cowboys—Wellington boots, chamois jackets, work shirts, and wheat jeans; the roaring motorcycle engine, though not quite domesticated, became a gleaming nickel-plate banjo or fine hand-crafted mahogany guitar. Much of Beat culture survived in the folk revival, too: the coffee house, existentialist philosophy, symbolist poetry, and the rest. This was the world, as one commentator put it, of "barren lofts, damp cellars, bearded men, candles in bottles, wine, free love, intellectuals, pseudo-intellectuals, and total disagreement with the Dale Carnegie system.[26] But jazz, as Alan Lomax put it, had "wandered into the harmonic jungles of Schönberg and Stravinsky,"[27] while a search for the primitive origins of jazz, begun years earlier by anthropologists and musicologists, had prepared the way in bohemian culture for folk music to enter and displace it. Jazz impresario John Hammond, a champion of racial integration in music and discoverer of Billie Holliday, Count Basie, and Charlie Christian, among others—had brought Alabama blues harmonica player Sonny Terry and Arkansas country blues singer Big Bill Broonzy to New York in 1938 for his historic "Spirituals to Swing" concert at Carnegie Hall. And in 1962, Hammond convinced skeptical Columbia executives to sign Bob Dylan, whose first album he produced.[28]

The triumph of Bob Dylan's first album was a triumph for all. Playing the desperado, the tramp, the poet, the peasant, or the earth mother had been nursed and protected by the college campus and sanctioned by the broad complicity of one's peers; now it was conspicuously ratified by the commercial establishment. Play had become an instrument for shaping reality and hence a means of laying claim to the social and historical initiative. This was the contribution of the folk revival to the counterculture, which, with its coherence, its relative freedom from social and economic constraints, and—above all—its youthfulness, acquired an enchanted, primitive, tribal quality that carnivalized the existing world with roles rooted in the imaginative life. Like all things imaginative, these roles urged their own actualization.

All this had begun in the 1950s, when Hollywood idols such as Marlon Brando and James Dean made heroes of the teenagers hanging around the soda fountain and cruising the streets on motorcycles, or of the brooding sons and daughters who could neither understand nor were understood by their parents. James Dean—restless but not warlike, with more than a trace of Steinbeck's Tom Joad in him—was, perhaps, the transitional figure. Interestingly, *Rebel Without a Cause* was directed by Nicholas Ray, a populist and folk song enthusiast closely associated, in the 1940s, with Alan Lomax, Woody Guthrie, and Pete Seeger.[29]

This subtle drift of the cultural center—from Brando to Dean, Zimmerman to Dylan—seems to reflect a deeper shift in the strata of our cultural life. The Hell's Angel aboard his motorcycle recalls, and perhaps descends from, the Ringtail Roarer, the fiercely independent Scots-Irish frontiersman of Old Kentucky; but the sandy-haired, solitary son of the California grower that we saw in *East of Eden* descends from the egalitarian West, with its family-bound and community-building immigrant pioneers from central and northern Europe. One is wild and will not be contained in representations—he becomes James Fenimore Cooper's noble savage, minstrelsy's cartoon, or Hollywood's misfit; the other abides with the possible in Willa Cather and John Steinbeck. One is parochial, born out of regional America, at once hallowed and despised; the other is public, the symbol of an American nation. In short, the movement from one to the other signifies the evolution of an idea written into our founding documents, the idea of the People, with which in each epoch we seek to reinvent ourselves. For the counterculture it was a figurative westward migration to the Promised Land, which ultimately became, in Haight-Ashbury, as literal as Israel.

Folk song, shaped over time by the life of a people, sends its influences out of itself to shape life anew. Well after the commercial popularity of folk song had faded, many diehard revivalists, becoming now parents and householders, endeavored, after the cataclysms of the 1960s, to create a life somehow compatible with the essential message of folk song—a life of deliberation, resourcefulness, and strict economy as distinctly American as Thoreau's Walden Pond. Chickens and goats, cottage crafts, organic gardening, home canning and preserving, wood heating, natural foods, natural fibers, natural childbirth—though inflation undercut most of these experiments, or sent them along commercial routes into exurbia to occupy the weekends of the rich, they were the late contributions to American life by young adults for whom folk music had become, in Barbara Kirshenblatt-Gimblett's phrase, "the site of resistance to the centralization of power"—not only of economic power, of course, but of cultural power.[30] Some, like conservatory-trained Andy Cahan, who left Oberlin for Low Gap, North Carolina, to apprentice himself to the great old-time fiddler and banjo player Tommy Jarrell, have adopted not only the music of their mentors but their way of life—its having been at last understood that only from a way of life can folk music, or any music, genuinely proceed. It has become a joke, in fact, that Galax, Virginia, string bands now traditionally carry a Jewish banjo player from Brooklyn or Queens.

Through the folk revival the broad typology of the American character, and with it the principle of cultural democracy, long established in literature, journalism, theater, film, and elsewhere—what Kenneth Rexroth called "the old free America"—

sought a new apotheosis on the social landscape.[31] The "old free America" was, of course, an artifact, too, of the cultural imagination—but without it we have only a winter of naked "society" in which to live. It had emerged on the minstrel stage and in regionalist journalism and literature, in tent-shows, vaudeville, and Hollywood film, out of the traffic in human encounter that transpires across the intricate network of America's social boundaries, particularly those that lie between urban and provincial cultures. In Melville and Whitman, it ascended from the comic to the heroic, and in the New Deal era, it proliferated in guidebooks, photographs, field recordings of folk songs and oral history, theater, dance, painting, The Index of American Design, all of which strove not only to document the scenes, the faces, the music, and the art of the American people, but to embody the American character in cultural heroes such as Abraham Lincoln or Woody Guthrie, the "dustbowl balladeer." Via his friend and follower Pete Seeger, Woody Guthrie influenced hundreds of young people in schools, colleges, and summer camps throughout the 1950s. Even after Guthrie disappeared from Washington Square hootenannies due to his lengthy and fatal illness, his figure survived to shape the personas of numberless young balladeers, including, of course, Bob Dylan—who in his touching "Song to Woody" placed him among the folk heroes who had "come with the dust and are gone with the wind."

From our vantage point of 25 years, we can detect in the folk revival the undercurrents of race, social class, and sheer money working to carry the influences of the northeastern cultural establishment into broad circulation in the wider republic, along the channels of a giant entertainment industry flowing as ever in America with democratic optimism and class aspiration. The supreme moment in the national seance of the folk revival was the Newport Folk Festival of 1963: the summons of folk song to the cultural dead populated the stage with a reunited family of American archetypes, not as costumes or masks but, either by nature or

Peter, Paul, and Mary; Joan Baez; Bob Dylan; the Freedom Singers; and Pete Seeger at the Newport Folk Festival, 1963. Photo: David Gahr. Courtesy of David Gahr.

by art, as genuine incarnations. While "thousands of fans milled in the darkened streets outside, listening to the music drift over the stone walls of the arena," Pete Seeger, Bob Dylan, Joan Baez, and Peter, Paul and Mary linked arms with the Student Nonviolent Coordinating Committee's Freedom Singers to sing the festival's closing songs of freedom, peace, and hope.[32] It was a moment in which, like a celestial syzygy, many independent forces of tradition and culture, some of them in historical deep space and others only transient displays in the contemporary cultural atmosphere, briefly converged to reveal, though inscrutably, the truth of our national life. Peter, Paul and Mary, for example, might have flourished on the Christian Missionary Youth circuit, though they were as ecumenical as a chocolate bar.

Among this group of people, Woody Guthrie was, of course, present in spirit, as was Johnny Appleseed, to whom Pete Seeger had aptly compared himself. But also present in spirit in the Freedom Singers were the Fisk Jubilee Singers of the 1870s; and in Pete Seeger, the Alamancs, labor songsters of the 1940s. Joan Baez might have been a dark Pocahontas; but she recalled, too, a demure Convent School girl, singing an Elizabethan ballad and dreaming of its hero, a dashing Gypsy Laddie-o. Others, more dim, lingered around the group—a Calvinist, Yankee man of the cloth; a Jehovah's Witness; a blackface minstrel with a banjo, and a yeshiva boy—all of them held together with the vast chorus of the audience in the parables of Dylan's "Blowin' in the Wind," and the sweet dreams of the old Baptist hymn, anthem of the Civil Rights movement, "We Shall Overcome."

NOTES

1. Bob Dylan, "From a Buick 6," on Bob Dylan, *Highway 61 Revisited*, Columbia 2389, 1965.
2. Bob Dylan, "Highway 61 Revisited," on *Highway 61 Revisited*.
3. B. A. Botkin, president of the American Folklore Society, at the national convention of music teachers in 1944 had called for the use of folk song in elementary music education. Note, *Journal of American Folklore* 57 (1944): 215.
4. Oscar Brand, *The Ballad Mongers* (New York: Funk & Wagnall's, 1962) p. 84.
5. For this statistic on the baby boom, I am indebted to Barbara Franco of the Museum of Our National Heritage—but more deeply indebted to her for the incentive to distinguish the folk revivalists as a group from the larger youth culture that emerged in the 1960s.
6. Alan Lomax, "The 'Folkniks'—and the Songs They Sing," *Sing Out!* 9 (Summer 1959): 30–31.
7. Paul Nelson, "Newport: Down There on a Visit," *Little Sandy Review* 30 (1965): 53.
8. These images all come from Elvis Presley's RCA Victor recordings of 1956: "Heartbreak Hotel," "Hound Dog," and "My Baby Left Me." But they belong to the idiom of traditional blues.
9. My account of the origins of "Tom Dooley" follows Anne Warner's in *Traditional American Folksongs from the Anne and Frank Warner Collection* (Syracuse, N.Y.: Syracuse University Press, 1984), pp. 251–261.
10. John A. and Alan Lomax, *Folk Song U.S.A.* (N.Y.: Duell, Sloan & Pearce, 1947).
11. David King Dunaway, *How Can I Keep from Singing: Pete Seeger* (New York: McGraw-Hill), p. 194.
12. Seeger had first published *How-to-Play the 5-String Bango* in mimeograph, in 1948.
13. Belafonte had begun his career as a folksinger in 1948 at New York Town Hall, where he played the role of the southern preacher in the cantata *The Lonesome Train*, a tribute to Abraham Lincoln written by the Popular Front composer Earl Robinson and Almanac Singer Millard Lampell in 1940. Dunaway, *How Can I Keep From Singing*, p. 140.
14. See Charles K. Wolfe, *Tennessee Strings: The Story of Country Music in Tennessee* (Knoxville: University of Tennessee Press, 1977), pp. 46–47.

15. See Ibid. The account of Rinzler's visit to North Carolina is a summary of his own, from an interview with the author on January 19, 1986.

16. Rinzler's name, incidentally, had been suggested to James Morris, director of the Smithsonian's Division of Performing Arts, by Joe Hickerson, now director of the Archive of Folk Culture at the Library of Congress; the occasion was a memorial gathering in Washington for the man who nearly 30 years earlier had given away a song—Frank Proffitt. See author's interview with Joe Hickerson, March 31, 1988.

17. Dunaway, *How Can I Keep from Singing*, 105.

18. Carl Sandburg, *American Songbag* (New York: Harcourt, Brace & Co., 1927), *ix*.

19. Quoted by Susan Montgomery, "The Folk Furor," *Mademoiselle* (December 1960): 118.

20. Ibid.

21. Ibid., p. 99.

22. Nelson, "Newport," p. 51.

23. John Cohen, "In Defense of City Folksingers," *Sing Out!* 9 (Summer 1959): 33–34.

24. Montgomery, "The Folk Furor," 118.

25. Anthony Scaduto, *Bob Dylan: An Intimate Biography* (New York: Grosset & Dunlap, 1971).

26. Ed Sherman, liner notes in LP, *Alan Lomax Presents: Folk Song Festival at Carnegie Hall* United Artists, 1959.

27. "Bluegrass Background: Folk Music with Overdrive," *Esquire* 52 (October, 1959): 108.

28. See "John Hammond, Critic and Discoverer of Pop Talent, Dies," *New York Times*, July 11, 1987, p. 1 & 17.

29. Joe Klein, *Woody Guthrie: A Life* (New York: Ballantine, 1980), p. 206.

30. Barbara Kirschenblatt-Gimblett, "Mistaken Dichotomies," *Journal of American Folklore* 101, 400 (April–June 1988): 151.

31. In John Cohen, "Roscoe Holcomb at Zabriski Point" *Sing Out!* 20 (September–October 1970): 20–21, quoting from Kenneth Rexroth's *New York Times* review of Sandburg's letters.

32. Cheryl Anne Brauner, *A Study of the Newport Folk Festival and the Newport Folk Foundation* (Unpublished thesis, Dept. of Folklore, Memorial University of Newfoundland, 1983) 86–87.

Contributors

Roger D. Abrahams, professor of folklore and folklife at the University of Pennsylvania, is coordinator for the American Folklore Society's centennial activities in 1988 and a past president of the AFS. His numerous publications include *Deep Down in the Jungle: Negro Narrative Folklore from the Streets of Philadelphia* (1970), *The Man-of-Words in the West Indies* (1983), and *When I Was Young, I Could Sing a Song: Almeda Riddle's Life and Songs* (in press).

Jane S. Becker, project coordinator for the exhibition, is a doctoral candidate in American Studies at Boston University. She participated in the NEH-funded exhibit, "The Art That is Life: The Arts and Crafts Movement in America, 1875–1920," at the Museum of Fine Arts, Boston, and contributed to the exhibition catalogue. She has worked at a number of museums and historical agencies, including the Museum of American Textile History and the Essex Institute.

Dillon Bustin, folklife and ethnic arts coordinator for the Massachusetts Council on the Arts and Humanities, has made several documentary films about folklife in southern Indiana and has extensive experience producing festivals of traditional music and developing curricula for public schools. He is also a banjo player, dance caller, and ballad singer, and the author of *If You Outdie Me: A Study of Modernization and Folk Culture in Southern Indiana* (1983) and *Maid of Ashes: Indiana Folk Artist Lois Doane* (in press).

Robert Cantwell, visiting associate professor, Georgetown University, is also scholar/writer at the Office of Folklife Programs, Smithsonian Institution, where he is studying the history of the Festival of American Folklife. His publications include *Bluegrass Breakdown: The Making of the Old Southern Sound* (1984).

Rayna Green is director of the American Indian Program, National Museum of American History, Smithsonian Institution, and a member of the Cherokee Nation of Oklahoma. She has published in journals and written for television and film, including the script for *More Than Bows and Arrows*. A former president of the American Folklore Society, she has worked extensively with tribes and federal and private agencies to improve tribal scientific and technical capabilities.

ALAN JABBOUR is president of the American Folklore Society and director of the American Folklife Center at the Library of Congress. A folklorist and concert violinist, he became interested in American fiddle styles and published the recordings *American Fiddle Tunes* and *The Hammons Family: A Study of a West Virginia Family's Traditions* (1973) under the aegis of the Archive of Folk Song at the Library of Congress. As director of the American Folklife Center, he has worked closely with other federal and state programs involved in the conservation of cultural resources.

T. J. JACKSON LEARS, professor of history, Rutgers University, is the author of *No Place of Grace: Antimodernism and the Transformation of American Culture, 1880–1920* (1981) and co-editor of *The Culture of Consumption: Critical Essays in American History 1880–1980* (1983). He is working on a book on the relationships between American advertising and American culture since the mid-19th century. He also serves on the editorial board of the *Journal of American History*.

EUGENE W. METCALF, JR., associate professor of interdisciplinary studies, Miami University, is the author of *Paul Laurence Dunbar: An Annotated Bibliography* (1975) and co-author with Curtis W. Ellison of *William Wells Brown and Martin Delany* (1978) and *Charles W. Chestnutt* (1977). He was guest curator for the exhibit, "The Ties that Bind: Folk Art and Modern American Culture," sponsored by the Cincinnati Contemporary Art Museum, for which he organized the first national conference on contemporary folk art.

CLAUDINE WEATHERFORD is assistant dean of social sciences, arts, and humanities at the University of Maryland/University College. Her publications include *The Art of Queena Stovall: Images of Country Life* (1986). She was guest curator for an exhibition of Queena Stovall paintings at the Maier Museum of Art, Lynchburg, Virginia.

Meriden-Stinehour Press, Lunenburg, Vermont